Michael Macintyre

THE SHOGUN INHERITANCE

JAPAN AND THE LEGACY OF THE SAMURAI

COLLINS
BRITISH BROADCASTING CORPORATION
1981

To Marianne

Published by William Collins Sons and Co Ltd
London · Glasgow · Sydney · Auckland · Toronto · Johannesburg
and the British Broadcasting Corporation
35 Marylebone High Street, London W1M 4AA

First published 1981
© Michael Macintyre 1981

Macintyre, Michael
   The Shogun inheritance.
   1. Japan – History
   I. Title
   952   DS835

ISBN 0-00-216350-0 Collins
ISBN 0-563-17942-2 BBC

Set in Monophoto Sabon by MS Filmsetting Ltd, Frome
Origination by New Interlitho SpA, Milan
Printed and Bound in Italy
by New Interlitho SpA, Milan

CONTENTS

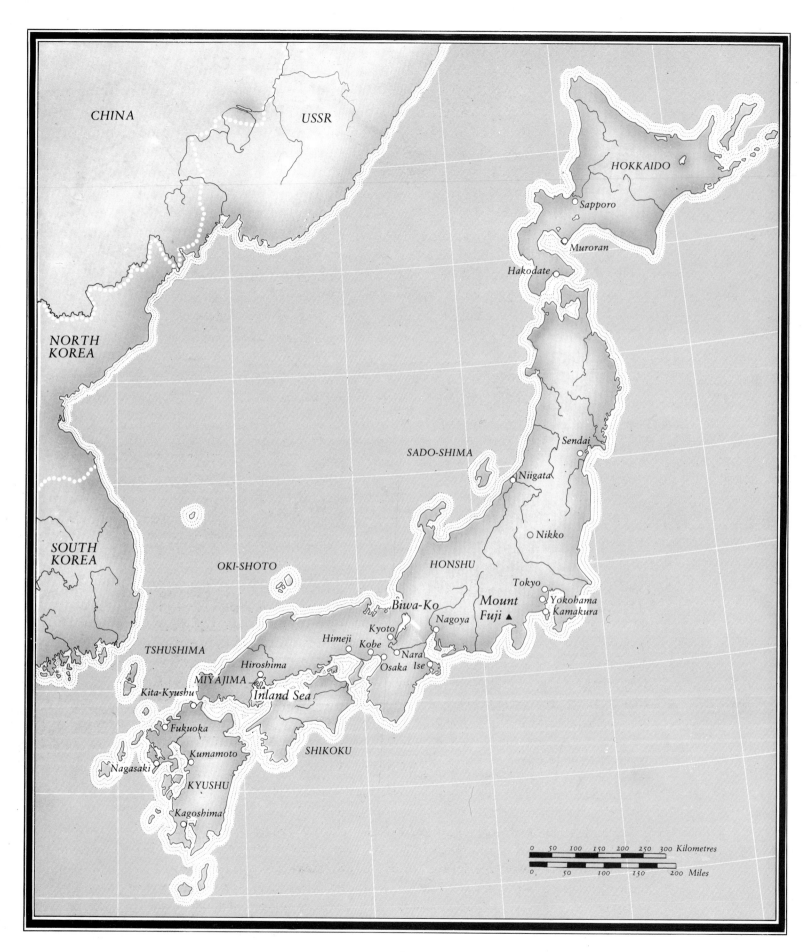

CHINA

USSR

HOKKAIDO

Sapporo

Muroran

Hakodate

NORTH
KOREA

SADO-SHIMA

Sendai

Niigata

SOUTH
KOREA

OKI-SHOTO

HONSHU

Nikko

Tokyo

Mount
Fuji ▲

Yokohama
Kamakura

Biwa-Ko

Nagoya

TSHUSHIMA

Kyoto

Kobe

Himeji

Nara

Osaka

Ise

Hiroshima

MIYAJIMA

Kita-Kyushu

Inland Sea

Fukuoka

SHIKOKU

Kumamoto

Nagasaki

KYUSHU

Kagoshima

| 0 | 50 | 100 | 150 | 200 | 250 | 300 Kilometres |

| 0 | 50 | 100 | 150 | 200 Miles |

INTRODUCTION

On 8 July 1853, the 'Black Ships' of the American Commodore Perry entered the Bay of Edo and forced an end to the policy of seclusion which, for two hundred years, had effectively isolated Japan from the rest of the world. They carried a message from the President of the United States requesting the opening of trade, and Perry made it clear that he would be returning the following spring with a larger fleet, and that the Japanese would be wise to accept the American proposition without delay. He had arrived at an opportune moment. The military ruler of Japan, the 'shogun' or 'Barbarian-conquering Great General', no longer possessed the strength to defy barbarians as his ancestors had done in the days of Kublai Khan, and already the feudal system, by which the country had been governed for nearly a millennium, was crumbling, unable to accommodate a merchant class which had grown prosperous. A few years later the shogunate was overthrown, feudalism was abolished, and Japan entered the modern age.

But the Japanese were not easily to shake off the influence of the past, and many of them had no wish to do so. The new Japan was characterized by a blending of Western technology with Japanese spirituality, and even today, a hundred years later, the feudal attitudes persist and continue to exercise control over virtually every aspect of Japanese life. At work and at play, in the most formal situations and in the most relaxed, the Japanese are, to a remarkable degree, the slaves of conventions established long ago, in times of warlords and 'samurai', when everyone knew his place and every aspect of daily life was circumscribed by a most rigid code of conduct dictated from above. This is the 'Shogun Inheritance' of our title, and it is the purpose of this book to illustrate the debt which modern Japan owes to the past.

The Japanese have a deep respect for antiquity, and throughout history they have sought to protect and preserve their ancient native institutions, and defend them from contamination by the world at large. Hirohito, the present Japanese emperor, belongs to a family line which stretches back unbroken for nearly two thousand years, by far the most ancient ruling lineage in the world. His musicians in the Imperial Court Orchestra are custodians of 'gagaku', the world's oldest orchestral music which dates back to the T'ang dynasty of seventh-century China, and which has been preserved within the families of the musicians as an inherited privilege through thirteen centuries.

As with living traditions, so with the material evidence of past glories. In the old capital of Nara stands the Shosoin, a repository of 100,000 precious objects collected together in the eighth century. Since that time the building has rarely been opened, and its timbers have protected the contents against extremes of temperature and humidity, so that today they survive in a remarkable state of preservation. Even older, the Grand Shrine at Ise has stood in its present form for more than seventeen centuries, though in not precisely the same materials. Every twenty years it has been rebuilt, so as perpetually to appear as new, but the task of the builders has always been to make an exact copy of the previous structure and thus preserve the divinely inspired perfection of the original.

This desire for continuity has had a profound effect on the course of Japan's history, which has been characterized by gradual development and slow change. From the sixth century onwards, there was no appreciable immigration, no foreign blood to taint the purity of the Japanese race, and until the Americans arrived at the end of the Pacific war, no foreign occupation. During a period of nearly a hundred years (1542–1640), Portuguese and Spanish missionaries were admitted to the country, an Englishman was adopted by the shogun as adviser on Western affairs, and a Dutch trading centre was established at Nagasaki. Otherwise, the Japanese were left to their own devices, and, for more than a thousand years, to run their country without let or hindrance of foreign intervention.

Not surprisingly, Japanese culture took on a strong character of its own, distinct even from that of China, its close and most influential neighbour. Japan's earliest written script came from China, as did its city planning, Buddhist religion, architecture, and a sophisticated repertoire of music and dance. But Japan was never colonized by China. It adopted whatever it needed or admired, and pragmatically grafted the foreign elements onto its own existing order. Thus Buddhism, which originated in India, spread to China in the first century and thence to Japan in the sixth, did not then displace the native faith of Shinto. Instead, the two religions were made to complement each other and serve different needs in the lives of the people. The Japanese, lacking any comprehensive moral philosophy of their own, were, and still are, remarkably open-minded towards other cultures, and able to borrow from them with no loss of pride, and without in any way losing their own distinctive personality.

Today the cities of Japan show to the world a Western face. Elevated expressways wind their way between high-rise office buildings and the crowded apartment blocks of residential areas. Businessmen, dressed in Western suits and carrying Western umbrellas, climb into taxis and crowd onto commuter trains. Children go to school in Western-style uniforms, satchels on their backs. Shops display the latest fashions from Paris and restaurants bear European names. Model girls undergo plastic surgery to make their eyes rounder, and they decorate the streets with giant posters which differ from those of the West only in their calligraphy. The people eat hamburgers, play golf and baseball and 'Space Invaders', and spend their evenings in bars and discos, where they listen almost exclusively to Western music.

And yet, the feeling is not Western at all. The businessmen are too well disciplined to be Western. They stand in discreet lines ready to enter a particular door of the commuter train, which they know will open directly in front of them. The trains are too well-timed to be Western, being run with the split-second accuracy of the computer. The children are too obedient, and will never cross an empty street if the pedestrian light is at red. The taxis are too clean to be Western, with their white cotton seat covers and collection of cloths, buckets and feather dusters, which they always carry in the boot. Even at play the Japanese are instantly recognizable by their energy and single-minded attention to the task facing them.

These patterns of behaviour are signs of fundamental and profound differences between Japan and the West in the basic ordering of their societies. In Japan there is respect for authority, and an overridingly strong feeling for hierarchy. Everyone is conscious of his status and place in life, and of loyalties and obligations to those above and below him. The interests of the group are always placed before those of the individual, but decisions within the group are reached by consensus so that no one loses face by being overruled or outvoted. Japanese industrial companies are, by Western standards, remarkably paternalistic, offering their workers lifelong security of employment, cheap housing, organized holidays, and even choosing for them suitable wives. Loyalty to the company is so strong that workers tend to take less holiday time than they are due, little production is lost through strikes, and relatively few ever leave the company to seek advancement elsewhere. When these factors are coupled with the prodigious energy of the Japanese and the up-to-date mechanization of their assembly lines, it is hardly surprising that they have become, in so short a time, the world's third industrial nation.

The social attitudes of modern Japan have been long in the making and they represent the sum total of Japanese experience during more than two thousand years, but it is reasonable to suppose that the most recent period of feudalism exerted more influence on the Japanese character than any other, because it was in this, the Edo period of 1603–1868 (named after the capital, which later became Tokyo), that standards of behaviour were rigidly enforced by the Tokugawa shoguns and the feudal lords who owed them allegiance, and everyone was obliged to live as befitted his particular station within the hierarchy. Even the clothes he wore, his food, and the kind of house he lived in, were dictated by the shogunate, and he was required to post on his doorway the details of his hereditary family status.

At the pinnacle of the hierarchy during this period was the emperor, but his role was ceremonial and symbolic – the real power lay with the shogun, the military leader who, tradition decreed, could emerge only from the ranks of the Minamoto clan. At the end of the sixteenth century, three great generals – Nobunaga, Hideyoshi, and Ieyasu – had succeeded in uniting the country after a hundred years of fighting among the provincial warlords. In 1603 Ieyasu, possessing the good fortune to outlive his two comrades at arms, and claiming descent from the Minamoto, was able to have himself appointed shogun by the emperor, and transfer the seat of government from Kyoto to

9

his own castle town of Edo. A man of cunning and foresight, he had, within a few years, eliminated all serious contenders for supreme power and laid the foundations for two hundred and fifty years of peace under the continuing rule of his own family line, the Tokugawa.

Tokugawa society was ordered in accordance with the Chinese philosophy of Neo-Confucianism, based on the Confucian classics written some two thousand years earlier. In these were listed the principles which, to Confucius, constituted ethical conduct, and prominent among them were reverence for the past, submissiveness to the established customs, and submissiveness to authority. The shoguns used these principles to justify and enforce their privileged status, and to dictate rules of behaviour to everyone else. Next in rank to the shogun were some three hundred barons, the 'daimyo', each of whom controlled territories of varying sizes with the aid of his samurai retainers. Below the samurai were the farmers, feudal subjects of the daimyo, then the artisans, and at the bottom of the scale of privilege, the merchants. Still below these were 'classless' people – actors, courtesans, beggars, the blind, and the eta who buried the dead and manned the abattoirs – 'people one does not mention but to whom kindness must be shown', in the words of Ieyasu.

This, to the Confucian way of thinking, was the natural order of things, and it was the duty of everyone to accept his lot with a good grace, and obey his superiors without question. Particular emphasis was placed on the loyalty and obedience owed by a son to his father, by a wife to her husband, by a younger brother to an older, by one friend to another, and by a subject to his ruler. Thus it was an imported Chinese philosophy rather than an innately Japanese one, which was used to legitimize the Edo class structure.

Ieyasu clearly saw himself as a man of destiny, and he was quick to consolidate his control of the nation with a series of legislative measures aimed at further curbing the power of the daimyos. Checkpoints were established at the borders of individual fiefs to watch for 'outgoing women and incoming guns', and so contain any possible threat of armed insurrection. Shogunate spies kept him informed of the accumulation of wealth, and any daimyo who showed signs of growing rich was invited to contribute generously towards the fortification of Edo castle. Most effective of all was the system of 'alternate attendance', whereby every daimyo was obliged to spend half of his time in Edo, and to leave behind his wife and children as potential hostages when he returned to his fief.

To ensure that everyone was suitably aware of correct behaviour, Ieyasu published, in 1615, the *Buke Sho-hatto*, a code of regulations, for the benefit of military families, together with a set of laws for the court nobles. For the military:

Drinking parties must be kept within proper limits ... Devotion to women and gambling is the primary cause of loss of one's fief ... There is to be no intercourse with the people of other fiefs outside one's own province ... Marriages must not be privately arranged ... There must be no confusion about the materials used for costume ... There must be a clear distinction between lord and vassal, superior and inferior ... Ordinary soldiers have taken to wearing figured material and brocade, a thing quite contrary to ancient rule and very objectionable ... The common herd are not to ride in palanquins ... Samurai of all fiefs are to practise economy. (1)*

And for the nobles:

The Court Nobles shall apply themselves to their studies with all diligence, both by day and night ... Guard duty must be performed by young and old, and not neglected ... It is strictly forbidden to them to go strolling about the streets and lanes of the city in places where they have

*References appear on page 214

no business . . . Except at public entertainments they are not to indulge in improper competitive games, and they are not to keep in their households worthless young samurai and the like.(1)

A year after his death Ieyasu's spirit was deified as 'Tosho Daigongen', 'Great Eastern illuminating Manifestation of Divinity', and enshrined within the Toshogu mausoleum on Mount Nikko. The 'Ieyasu Legacy' became endowed with the authority of holy writ, a most powerful source of inspiration for the generations which followed. It was very much in keeping with the wishes of Ieyasu that his grandson Iemitsu published, in 1642, a code of conduct for the peasants, further emphasizing the rigid class distinctions of Tokugawa society:

As to the peasant's food. They must eat mixed grain. They certainly must not eat much rice. This must be made quite clear to them . . . The law allows only a Shoya or a Headman to wear coarse silk or pongee, and the ordinary farmer linen and cotton. In addition, no cravats are to be worn . . . No farmer or Shoya may dye any of his clothes red or pink. Moreover, whatever be the colours he must not dye them in patterns . . . It is forbidden to put a blanket on the pack saddle when riding it . . . Any combination of persons, for whatever purpose, shall be unlawful . . . Expenditure on religious festivals and Buddhism shall be in accordance with one's position . . .(1)

It was Iemitsu who, in 1640, effectively closed off the country with his policy of seclusion, a measure intended to consolidate the control of the Tokugawa family and deny the merchant class the opportunity to enrich itself by overseas trade. In time, the merchants too were to have their code of behaviour, the 'Way of the Chonin' (townspeople), by which they were urged to conduct their trade with diligence and honesty, and with unquestioning loyalty to the company.

In spite of the policies of Iemitsu and the shoguns who followed him, the outstanding feature of the late Edo period was the rise of the merchants from the lowest of the four class divisions, to a position where even the daimyo were obliged to treat them with respect. The economy had changed from one in which wealth was measured in terms of 'koku' – approximately, the quantity of rice a samurai would eat in a year – to one based on a currency in copper, silver and gold. It was considered inappropriate for the samurai elite to soil their hands with the base financial transactions of the common people – these matters were left to the merchants who, in consequence, prospered greatly. Many samurai and daimyo became indebted to moneylenders, to such a degree that, from time to time, the shogun was obliged to declare some such debts null and void, in order to ensure the survival of the traditional social order. Nevertheless, in keeping with the Japanese respect for hereditary institutions, the status of samurai remained high, and rich merchants considered it worthwhile to buy their way into the ranks of the élite, or have their son marry the daughter of a samurai in return for a cancelled debt.

By the close of the era, the social order had been greatly modified, and the merchant class had become exploitive rather than exploited. When the country opened its doors to the West, there was already a thriving business community ready to take advantage of the new opportunities of world trade, and already the beginnings of the Zaibatsu, the giant family conglomerates – later to be known under such names at Mitsui, Mitsubishi and Sumitomo – with their diversified interests in banking, insurance and heavy industry, and considerable influence in government circles.

In 1868 feudalism was abolished, but the samurai remained, and it was from among their number that the new government was formed, and on their guiding principles that the future depended.

I

SAMURAI

In November 1970, the death of Yukio Mishima astonished the world. Mishima, at forty-five, was the outstanding writer of his generation, the author of forty novels, eighteen plays, and twenty volumes of essays and short stories. Three times he had been nominated for the Nobel prize. But it was not the fact of his death so much as the manner of it which was astonishing, and it served as a vivid reminder that the ideals of the warrior élite of samurai still carried weight in modern Japan.

In the company of members of his private army, the Shield Society, Mishima went to the Tokyo headquarters of the Self-defence Force, and there held captive the commandant, whilst demanding the right to address the assembled regiment. At noon, he stepped out onto a balcony, and facing the eight hundred soldiers who had been hastily gathered together, exhorted them to join with him in putting an end to the postwar democracy 'which had deprived Japan of her army and her soul'. His words were greeted with jeers and hisses, and after only seven minutes, he returned to the commandant's office and there committed ritual suicide, 'harakiri', in the traditional samurai manner.

In passionately rejecting modern materialism, Mishima had turned increasingly to the past for his inspiration and spiritual identity, and had come to see himself as a latter-day samurai. Mishima was a compulsive reader but there was one book in particular which influenced him profoundly, and ultimately contributed to his death: this was *Hagakure*.

Literally translated 'Hidden among Leaves', *Hagakure* contains the teachings of Yamamoto Jocho, a samurai of the late seventeenth century who had been denied by new legislation the traditional privilege of ritual suicide after the death of his lord, and had become a priest recluse. Until the end of the feudal period, Jocho's teachings were kept a close secret by the daimyo of his domain in Kyushu, and they were used there for the instruction and inspiration of local samurai. Quite apart from the predictable exhortations to honour the liege lord and be filially pious, *Hagakure* includes these words of wisdom:

It is wrong to have strong personal convictions. If through diligence and concentration of mind a samurai acquires fixed opinions, he is apt to reach the hasty conclusion that he has already attained an acceptable level of performance; this is most inadvisable ... Until fifty or sixty years ago, samurai performed their ablutions every morning, shaved their heads, and perfumed their topknots. Then they cut their fingernails and toenails, filed them with pumice, and finally buffed them with kogane herb. Such fastidiousness may seem more trouble than it is worth, but it is what the Way of the Samurai is all about. One may be run through at any moment in vigorous battle; to die having neglected one's personal grooming is to reveal a general sloppiness of habit, and to be despised and mocked by the enemy... There is dignity in closeness of mouth. There is great dignity too in clenched teeth and flashing eyes ... A samurai should know his own stature, pursue his discipline with diligence, and say as little as possible ... A samurai must never drink too much, be overconfident, or indulge in luxury ... In times of peace it is language which manifests valour. A samurai must constantly be on guard lest he should let slip a word of weakness. From a slight remark uttered inadvertently, one's true nature may be guessed ... If a certain person wants to be considered a samurai, he must realize that any artistic accomplishment is a detriment to his samurai stature ... A samurai should make a habit of correcting his looks by observing himself in the mirror. What the daimyo dislikes above all else is a person who looks intelligent. A reverent yet stern, self-collected appearance is ideal ...(2)

Jocho's precepts were taken seriously by Mishima, who loved to be photographed in heroic poses and who, on the day of his death, wore a quotation from *Hagakure* on his headband. But Mishima gave his keenest attention to a less narcissistic section of the book, one which, during the Pacific war, was used to inspire 'kamikaze' pilots, as they set off on their suicide missions:

I discovered that the Way of the Samurai is death. In a fifty-fifty life or death crisis, simply settle it by choosing immediate death. There is nothing complicated about it. Just brace yourself and proceed. Some say that to die without accomplishing one's mission is to die in vain, but this is the calculating, imitation samurai ethic of arrogant Osaka merchants ... A samurai must take great pride in his military valour; he must have the supreme resolution to die a fanatic's death.(2)

It is not difficult to appreciate the usefulness of *Hagakure* as a propaganda weapon in wartime, and not surprising that it was quickly suppressed by the postwar government. But samurai legend and mythology had become so deeply ingrained in the national consciousness as to be irrepressible, and the samurai ethic lived on – in the spectacular festivals and processions which the Japanese love so much, in the plays of 'noh', 'kabuki' and 'bunraku', in the films of Akira Kurosawa (*The Seven Samurai, Throne of Blood, Kagemusha*) and, most pervasively, in the countless samurai drama serials which nightly occupy Japan's thirty million television screens.

Inevitably the samurai have been romanticized and idealized, and the Way of the Warrior has been adapted to suit the box office. There never was a blind swordsman who, like Zatoichi, could pinpoint a coin spinning in the air and instantly slice it in two, so that each half fell into a separate dish. But samurai history is rich nonetheless in heroism and adventure, which is at times even more remarkable than the mythology which surrounds it.

In prehistoric Japan between the third and the sixth centuries AD there was already a military élite, evidenced by the pottery figures of warriors, which surrounded the keyhole-shaped tombs of tribal chieftains. In the seventh and eighth centuries, the balance of power shifted in favour of the court nobility and a relatively effete way of life, but the military were always in attendance, and particularly influential in provincial districts. One of these was the Kanto region, of which Tokyo is now a part, but in the tenth century it was rugged frontier country where warring chieftains struggled for ascendancy over their neighbours. In time, individual fighting groups joined forces and established alliances, and it was in this way that a distinct warrior class of samurai, 'those who serve', emerged, sometime during the eleventh century.

At first, the samurai lifestyle was rugged and tied to the land, and it stood in great contrast to the sophisticated luxury of court life in Kyoto. And yet, ironically, it was from Kyoto that the greatest samurai leaders were to come – from the princely families of the Taira and Minamoto who, by the early twelfth century, had become the principal contenders for military supremacy.

The conflict between the two samurai clans culminated in the famous Gempei war of 1180–85. In a series of battles distinguished by acts of heroism which have since become legendary, the Minamoto leader, Yoritomo, emerged victorious. The Gempei war did much to enhance the prestige of the samurai, and it took a powerful hold on the Japanese imagination, providing the inspiration for countless plays of noh and kabuki, and epic stories such as the *Heike Monogatari*, 'Tales of the Heike'. (Heike is another name for the Taira, just as Genji is the alternative of Minamoto.)

On achieving victory, Yoritomo established his seat of government at Kamakura in the Kanto, nearly four hundred miles from the Imperial Palace in Kyoto, and seven years later he became the first ruler of the country to bear the title of shogun. Yoritomo had chosen to distance himself from the emperor to be free of court intrigue and to underline what he saw to be the essential differences between the functions of the court and the shogunate. The emperor was to continue as the semidivine figurehead of the Japanese nation, and as the ultimate legitimizing power in all ceremonial affairs of the state. But the day-to-day running of the country came increasingly to rest in the hands of the military, the samurai, under the supreme leadership of the shogun. So began the medieval age of feudalism, which was to last until the start of the Edo period four hundred years later.

The early samurai were men of action, a rough breed of fighters highly skilled in the arts of swordsmanship, horsemanship and archery. They were renowned for their bravery and their ability to endure pain and suffering, and they lived by a most exacting code of behaviour in which the highest value was placed on loyalty to their lord. Those found guilty of disloyalty or other shameful conduct were normally given the chance to regain their lost honour by committing 'seppuku' (the more formal term for harakiri), an exceptionally painful form of ritual suicide which involved plunging a short sword into the stomach and drawing it sharply from left to right. The samurai were expected to endure this ordeal with total composure, uttering no sound and showing no sign of emotion whatsoever.

During the medieval period it had been possible for anyone to carry arms, but in 1588 Hideyoshi ordered a nationwide 'sword hunt':

The people of the various provinces are strictly forbidden to have in their possession any swords, short swords, bows, spears, firearms, or other types of arms ... Therefore the heads of provinces, official agents, and deputies are ordered to collect all the weapons mentioned above and turn them over to the government.

Swords and short swords thus collected will not be wasted. They shall be used as nails and bolts in the construction of the Great Image of Buddha. This will benefit the people not only in this life but also in the next...(3)

Naturally, this did not apply to the samurai, and from that time onwards only they were permitted to carry swords, whilst the peasants were left virtually defenceless. Not surprisingly, samurai were treated with the greatest deference and respect, and were addressed, if at all, from a lowly posture and in words of extreme humility and self-abasement.

The sword, the 'soul of the samurai', was his constant companion, and the symbol of his authority. Every samurai carried two swords – the long one, 'tachi', used in man-to-man combat, and the short one, 'wakizashi', used to commit seppuku. Though probably the most lethal swords ever invented, they were objects of beauty and much valued as works of art. Their blades were elegantly proportioned and gracefully curved, and the decoration on hand guard and hilt was often superbly executed in the most minute detail.

The making of a Japanese sword was attended by the rituals of Shinto, the native religion which requires the worship of 'kami', spirits of nature. Daily the swordsmith would undergo ritual purification and make offerings to the spirit shrine which stood beside his furnace. The intention was to endow the blade with magical properties which would bring a long and distinguished life to its owner, but in using his sword, many of the samurai sought assistance from another religion – that of Zen Buddhism. The practice of Zen, 'meditation', aims at ascetic self-discipline and the concentration of willpower, so that the individual is capable of purposeful action, his mind uncluttered by philosophical speculation as to whether his action may be right or wrong, or as to its consequences. The swordsman who acts in the spirit of Zen, acts instinctively, with his mind in the state of 'munen', 'no-thought', and therefore oblivious as to whether he is facing victory or death. The capacity to fight in this way, and channel their already impressive energies into single-minded action was to earn for the samurai a reputation as the most formidable fighters in Asia, 'a people so desperate and daring that they are feared in all places where they come'.

In the Middle Ages the samurai made frequent use of their swords, for these were the times of heroism and adventure so vividly portrayed in the films of Kurosawa. In 1274 and 1281 came the invading armies of Kublai Khan, repelled on both occasions after heavy fighting, and, on the second, with the divine assistance of Kamikaze, the 'Wind of the Gods'. In 1467 a dispute over the office of shogun led to the Onin war and the loss of authority of court and shogunate alike. The war marked the beginning of Sengoku, a hundred-year period of social upheaval and constant fighting as rival warlords struggled to increase their holdings and prestige. The final outcome of a century of bloodshed was the result not so much of bravery in battle, which could always be counted on, as of cunning and deception and uncompromising ruthlessness. In 1571 Oda Nobunaga was able to destroy three thousand monastery buildings and slaughter many thousands of monks as his first step towards supreme power. Thirty years later, Tokugawa Ieyasu achieved victory at the great battle of Sekigahara by arranging that a key figure on the opposing side would defect at a critical moment in the fighting. In the decisive campaigns against Osaka castle in the winter of 1614 and spring of 1615, Ieyasu was again victorious through trickery, and he was so determined to protect his family line against any possible opposition in the future that he put to death a child of six, the grandson of Hideyoshi, his old comrade in arms. In the peaceful times which followed the fall of Osaka castle, the samurai were to find little opportunity to demonstrate their military skills, and many became demoralized and given to brawling and rowdy behaviour. This was especially true of the 'ronin', masterless samurai who often found themselves among the ranks of the unemployed. No longer did all samurai abide by the ancient unwritten code of loyalty and honourable conduct which had distinguished their forebears on the battlefield, and yet it was now ironically (or for that very reason) that 'bushido', the Way of the Warrior, came to be formalized as a code of behaviour, first by way of Ieyasu's *Buke Sho-hatto*, 'The Laws for Military Families', and later through the teachings of a Confucian scholar, Yamaga Soko:

It would not do for the samurai to know the martial and civil virtues without manifesting them. Outwardly he stands in physical readiness for any call to service and inwardly he strives to fulfil the Way of the lord and subject, friend and friend, father and son, older and younger brother, and husband and wife. Within his heart he keeps to the ways of peace, but without he keeps his weapons ready to use.(3)

The tea ceremony provided one of the rare occasions when the more exalted of the samurai were permitted to unburden themselves of their swords and forget, for a while, their duties and obligations. To enter the tearoom the samurai was obliged to bow low, the symbolic gesture of humility (the door was never more than three feet in height), and inside there were no distinctions between the guests, whether daimyo, samurai or commoner. This was no longer the stratified world of Confucianism, but the introspective, personal world of Zen, and the room itself was constructed with the austere simplicity of a Zen monastery. Here the samurai could allow his mind to relax into meditative calm, as he watched the hypnotically slow and precise actions of the tea master and listened to the water boiling in the iron kettle, 'as a distant sea breaking among the rocks, a rainstorm sweeping through a bamboo forest, or the soughing of pines on some far-away hill'.

As warfare became more and more a thing of the past, the tea ceremony increased in popularity and the samurai were gradually transformed into men of learning and cultural sophistication. They became painters, philosophers, historians, or worked as salaried officials within the rapidly growing bureaucratic administration. But whatever their calling, the samurai continued to carry their swords and maintain the social gulf between themselves and everyone else. Now that a military elite was no longer justified in practical terms, it was legitimized by the 'natural' division of classes in the Confucian social hierarchy, and great emphasis was placed on Confucian studies and on rigid adherence to the established codes of behaviour.

The Way of letters and arms, of archery and horsemanship, must be cultivated with all the heart and mind. In times of order we cannot forget disorder; how then can we relax our military training? The sword is the soul of the warrior. If any forget or lose it he will not be excused.'(1)

Ieyasu's words were not forgotten – the warrior class succeeded in outliving two hundred and fifty years of peace, and the samurai ethic survived, a ready source of inspiration for the military adventures of the future.

The Parade of A Thousand, Mount Nikko. In May 1617 the body of
Shogun Ieyasu was buried at Nikko in accordance with his wishes.
Ieyasu was the founder of the Tokugawa regime and his final resting
place became a centre of pilgrimage for his successors. The spectacular processions from Edo to Nikko have a modern counterpart
in the annual festival of Toshogu shrine. Before the grand parade
begins, the villagers dressed in samurai armour muster among the
shrine buildings, shaded by towering cryptomeria trees (*overleaf*).

Samurai armour was constructed of plates of metal or
bamboo held together with coloured lacing, and it was
intended to be elegant in appearance while still offering
protection from arrows and sword thrusts in battle.

A village samurai with his 'bento' lunch box.

During the samurai festival of Kaseda shrine on the
southern island of Kyushu, villagers fight with
sticks in place of the lethal samurai swords, but
they do not wear the masks and protective clothing
of 'kendo', and losing such a fight can be painful.

In the Middle Ages, samurai archers used techniques of
Zen meditation to concentrate willpower and free the
mind of distractions. The methods of Zen are still used
today, but at Kaseda archery is part of a festival not
of Buddhism, but of Shinto, the native religion of Japan.

A painting in the collection of the Shimazu daimyo family of Kagoshima. It shows a game of horseback archery using blunted arrows and a dog as a target.

'Yabusame' at the Hachimangu shrine in Kamakura. Horseback
archery has been a feature of the shrine's festival since
the early days of the Kamakura period (1192–1333), and this
rider is wearing a samurai costume of the thirteenth century.

'Sumo' is an ancient style of wrestling thought to have originated in Japan nearly 2000 years ago. The ring consists of a circle of clay set on a square mound, and a bout is decided when any part of a wrestler's body, except for the soles of his feet, touches the ground, or when he steps or is pushed out of the ring.

Previous pages Sumo wrestlers of the top division perform the 'dohyo-iri' (ring entry) ceremony, a preliminary to a Grand Championship fight.

Sumo has close associations with the Shinto religion; fights take place beneath a symbolic Shinto-style roof, and the wrestlers toss handfuls of salt (*opposite*) into the ring as an act of purification. The referee wears the costume of a shogun.

31

The sword was the 'soul of the samurai', and swordsmanship
was always a central feature of samurai training. At the
end of the feudal period, the samurai class was abolished,
and it became illegal to carry a sword in public. The art
of swordsmanship, 'kenjutsu', was transformed into the
sport of 'kendo', using swords of bamboo and guards to
protect the face. Real swords are still used in 'shinken',
a form of stylized combat against an imaginary opponent.

A member of the emperor's police guard performs
shinken in the dojo or gymnasium of the Imperial Palace.

The swordsmith Gassan Sadakazu is classified as a
'Human National Treasure', the only living swordmaker to bear
this honour. He is 73 years old, the heir to a
family tradition of swordmaking which goes back 800 years.
In feudal times the sword was more than a weapon – it was
the symbol of samurai potency, 'pure spirit moulded in
steel' – and swordsmiths were given high samurai status,
unlike other artisans who ranked lower than peasantry. Today
Master Gassan continues to use the traditional techniques
which, 800 years ago, produced the finest swords ever made.

The samurai film is the Japanese equivalent of the Western,
and it forms the staple diet of Japanese television.
In Tokyo and Kyoto large studios cater for the public
demand, turning out features and television drama serials
with the speed and efficiency of factory assembly lines.

Opposite An actor dressed as a samurai at the Toei
studios in Kyoto.

Above A small town of the Edo period (1603-1868)
reconstructed on a film set in Tokyo.

Actresses in the Toei studios prepare a scene for
a popular television series set in the Edo period.

Sen Soshitsu is the present Grand Tea Master of the Urasenke
Foundation in Kyoto, the head of an organization which currently
teaches the Way of Tea to some 8,000,000 people throughout the world.

Master Sen is a Zen abbot and the fifteenth-generation descendant
of Sen Rikyu, tea master to the great generals Nobunaga and
Hideyoshi, and the man responsible for the refined
simplicity of the tea ceremony as it is performed today.

The samurai class no longer exists, but there are still
samurai families who are proud of their ancestry, and
who continue to live in traditional samurai houses.

Here, in Chiran city on Kyushu, the home of the Mori
family clearly shows the influence of the tea ceremony
on domestic architecture. As in the tearoom, 'tatami'
matting covers the floor from wall to wall, and there is no
furniture and no decoration. Daylight enters diffusely
through door panels of rice paper, and the doors slide
open to reveal a small landscaped garden with rocks and
a pool. In everything, the emphasis is on refined simplicity
and the virtue of emptiness, and the inspiration is Zen.

The White Heron Castle of Himeji, the most beautiful of the feudal castles
of Japan, was built by Hideyoshi in 1581. Hideyoshi was a 'sengoku daimyo',
a 'civil war baron' who had worked his way up from the rank of foot soldier,
and he liked to celebrate his acquired status in surroundings of heroic splendour.

Opposite Five years after the building of Himeji, Hideyoshi completed Osaka
castle and rendered it virtually impregnable with a double moat and fortifying
walls of granite. Nevertheless, in 1615, after laying siege to the castle
over many weeks, Tokugawa Ieyasu succeeded in taking it by trickery, and in doing
so he removed the last vestiges of opposition to his regime. Ieyasu left
the outer walls in ruins, but the castle itself survived until 1860. The
present building is a reconstruction in ferroconcrete.

Overleaf The central donjon or keep of Himeji castle, known as 'tenshu-kaku',
'the high structure of the heavenly protector'.

2
MYSTERY IN NATURE

The natural beauty of Japan has been the inspiration of her artists and poets down the ages. Japanese landscape is mountainous, thickly wooded, and full of surprises. Contorted pines perch precariously on jagged pinnacles of rock, high waterfalls cascade through narrow gorges among forests of cedars and cypress – everywhere the land has been distorted and fragmented by the volcanic eruptions and earthquakes which created it, and it offers the eye an infinite variety of colours, shapes and textures, constantly changing through the year. The seasons are clearly marked, and each has a mood of its own. Spring brings cherry blossom, cheerful while it lasts, but with an intimation of sadness because it falls in its prime. Rhododendrons usher in the rainy season and an air of mystery and drama, as mountains and forests disappear in cloud and small streams become raging torrents. In autumn the rains subside, the hot springs fume and bubble in the sunshine, the chrysanthemums bloom, and the maple leaves turn a fiery red. In many ways this is the most pleasant time of the year, and the one most beloved of poets.

Mountains of volcanic origin occupy all but one fifth of the total land mass. The celebrated Mount Fuji is itself a volcano, and although it has been dormant for nearly three hundred years, it has many companions still rumbling and puffing smoke, and minor earthquakes are a daily occurrence. When one considers also that the country is prone to the heavy rains and mighty winds of typhoons, and to the devastation of

48

gigantic tidal waves caused by earth tremors beneath the sea, it might well be supposed that the people would regard nature with a respect born of terror, and that, in their shrines and temples, they would make offerings to placate the angry gods of earth, wind and ocean.

In fact, the Japanese do the reverse. Their respect for nature is profound, but it is based on delight, not fear, and Shinto, their religion of nature worship, is one of joy and affirmation, and offerings are made to thank the gods, not to appease their anger. The gods of Shinto, or more accurately the spirits, are called kami, and they are many and various:

A Kami may be a divine being, a mythical hero, a great sage or sovereign, a famous ancestor, but it may also be thunder, an echo in the forest, a fox, a tiger, a dragon. Perhaps we may imagine the universe animated by an all-pervading radiation: wherever this current attains a particular intensity, a higher temperature or voltage, revealing itself as beauty, power, wonder, there the ultimate becomes apparent: there is 'Kami'.(4)

In its primitive form two thousand years ago, Shinto appears to have entailed the recognition of some forty thousand kami, believed to reside in certain rocks, rivers, trees and mountains, and to influence the lives of those who dwelt in their domain. There were also the more powerful kami who controlled the elements – the wind and rain, the sun and moon, and the earth itself. In their worship the people set out to express gratitude for the beauty and abundance of their homeland, the 'Land of Fresh Rice Ears of a Thousand Autumns'. And they dedicated their most holy shrine, the Grand Shrine of Ise, not to a baleful god of earthquake, fire and tempest, but to Amaterasu O Mikami, the Sun Goddess, 'Heaven Shining Great August Deity'.

Above all, Shinto was concerned with the fertility of the land and ensuring a bountiful harvest, and the most important Shinto festivals were those which dealt with food. Every year, in the harvest festival, the gods were addressed in prayer and asked to send 'crops in ears long and in ears abundant, things growing in the great moor-plain, sweet herbs and bitter herbs, things that dwell in the blue sea-plain, the broad of fin and the narrow of fin, seawood from the offing, seaweed from the shore, clothing, bright stuffs and shining stuffs, coarse stuffs and fine stuffs'(5). More than anything else, the prosperity of the country depended on rice, and the rice god Inari enjoyed great popularity, being honoured with countless small shrines standing beside the rice fields. Each year in the festival of Ainame, 'Together Tasting', the emperor joined with the gods in sampling the new season's rice and the fresh brew of rice wine, 'sake', and throughout the year he personally tended a small rice paddy, symbolically re-enacting the sacred cycle of rice cultivation to ensure the future wellbeing of his people. Today, within the walls of the Imperial Palace in Tokyo, Emperor Hirohito continues to perform this ancient ritual.

The Grand Shrine of Ise was built sometime in the fifth century, a simple wooden structure of elegant proportions, nestling among tall trees and merging gracefully with its surroundings. Here, perhaps for the first time, the Japanese sensitivity to nature revealed itself in art, and established an ideal of refined simplicity which, a thousand years later, was to characterize the finest creations of Japanese architecture. By the sixth century, when Buddhism was imported from China by way of Korea, Shinto was already a vital force in Japanese culture, and its optimistic faith in the divinity of nature and of mankind (since the two were inseparable) persisted, and provided a reservoir of spiritual feeling from which artists and poets would continue to draw inspiration. The celebrated *Man'yoshu*, or 'Collection of Ten Thousand Leaves', is the oldest anthology of Japanese verse and contains 4500 poems, composed between the beginning of the seventh and the middle of the eighth centuries. It is enlivened by a passion and a down-to-earth directness which were later to disappear in the extreme refinement of court life.

The writing of the *Man'yoshu* in the mid-eighth century was made possible by the recent adoption of Chinese script – the Japanese had previously possessed no written language of their own, and poetry had existed purely as an oral tradition. Now, as Chinese culture of all kinds flooded into the country, the native taste for the simple and natural tended to be overpowered by pageantry and grandeur. In 752 the finishing touches were added to the Daibatsu, a gigantic statue of Buddha, 53 feet high and containing 3 million pounds of copper and 15,000 pounds of gold. To 'open the eyes' of the Buddha, a spectacular ceremony was held in the capital, Nara, and an assembly of guests from every corner of the Buddhist world were entertained with music and dancing.

Nara was built with the direct assistance of Chinese priests, mathematicians, architects and civil engineers, and today, immaculately preserved, it conveys the ghostly impression of an ancient Chinese city frozen in time. That it was able to survive in this way was because it was abandoned as the capital within a mere eighty years of its founding. In 784, seeking to place some distance between himself and the politically active Buddhist priesthood, the Emperor Kammu uprooted his court and transferred it to Nagoka and then, in 794, to Kyoto (Heian), where it was destined to remain for the better part of eleven hundred years.

During the first century of the Heian period (794–1185), official relations with China grew progressively weaker as the power of the T'ang court diminished, and, in 894, they were suspended altogether. The artistic traditions which had come from China were now virtually isolated from their roots, and gradually they became assimilated into Japanese cultural life and adapted to suit Japanese taste.

Freed of the cultural domination of China, and supported by the affluence of the nobility, the native arts took on a new lease of life, and the native taste for simplicity reasserted itself. In place of the sternly symmetrical and monumental architecture of China, the palace architects arranged their rooms asymmetrically around ponds and gardens, so that they would merge with the landscape, and they constructed them with unpainted woods and thatched roofs just as the builders of the Ise shrine had done five hundred years earlier.

Above all, the mid-Heian period was one of outstanding literary achievement, which was greatly assisted by the evolution of 'kana' syllabary, a simple phonetic script composed of abbreviated Chinese characters, each of which represented a single sound of the Japanese language. With kana it was now possible to write a poem with a few graceful strokes of the brush, instead of the many strokes per syllable required by the classic Chinese script, and the writing of Japanese verse took on new vigour and became in court circles the height of fashion.

'The poetry of Japan has its roots in the human heart and flourishes in the countless leaves of words ... It is poetry which, without exertion, moves heaven and earth, stirs the feeling of gods and spirits invisible to the eye, softens the relation between men and women, calms the hearts of fierce warriors.'

So ran the preface to the *Kokinshu*, published in 922, a collection of more than eleven hundred short poems which admirably convey the spirit of their time. They are composed with skill and finesse, and with a wealth of delicate and sensitive imagery, but they have little of the directness and emotional strength of the *Man'yoshu*, being limited in range by the dictates of courtly refinement. Poets of the Heian court were expected to express themselves only in such circumstances as 'when they looked at the scattered blossoms of a spring morning; when they listened of an autumn evening to the falling of leaves; when they sighed over the snow and waves reflected each passing year by their looking glasses; when they were startled into thoughts on the brevity of life by seeing the dew on the grass or the foam on the water; when, yesterday all proud and splendid, they have fallen from fortune into loneliness; or when, having been dearly loved, are neglected.'(6) Essentially, the poems of the *Kokinshu* are essays in refinement, and their authors were more concerned with polishing up a phrase to the point of perfection than with the expression of strong emotion.

The crowning achievement of the Heian period was not a poem but a novel, *Genji Monogatari*, 'The Tale of Genji', which is widely regarded as the supreme masterpiece of Japanese literature. It is the work of Murasaki Shikibu, a lady-in-waiting, and recounts the amorous adventures of 'the Shining Prince' Genji, accomplished poet, artist, musician, dancer, a man of dazzling good looks and impeccable good taste, the complete embodiment of Heian virtue. As Genji passes from one romantic encounter to another, he moves in a world of delicate beauty and subtle eroticism, the privileged, cloistered world of court society preoccupied with its own ideas of excellence and pervaded by a deeply felt mood of gentle melancholy, 'mono-no-aware'.

Genji's world was not the world of the samurai, and the values it extolled were in direct opposition to the self-denying austerity of the warrior code. The tranquillity of court life would soon be shattered by the clash of swords as Fujiwara gave way to Taira, and Taira to Minamoto, and the tales of the future would concern themselves with military glory and the noise of battle, rather than moonlight and the gently falling maple leaves of autumn.

The greatest of these war stories is *Heike Monogatari*, 'Tales of the Heike', an epic account of the rise and fall of the Taira (Heike) family and their virtual extermination at the hands of the Minamoto (Genji). The story resounds with heroism and military splendour, and it established for the first time the romantic ideal of the samurai. But the years of bloodshed left a legacy of gloom and disillusion, and the prevailing mood of the early medieval period was of an altogether darker and profounder melancholy than that which had brought pleasure to the Heian courtiers:

> In a tree standing
> Beside a desolate field,
> The voice of a dove
> Calling to its companions
> Lovely, terrible evening.
>
> (*New Kokinshu*, 1205) (7)

In place of the courtly refinement of miyabi, the poet now sought to convey 'yugen' – mystery or profundity, the inner meaning which lies behind appearances:

> When the floating bridge
> Of the dream of a spring night
> Was snapped, I woke:
> In the sky a bank of clouds
> Was drawing away from the peak.(7)

In 1334, the Kamakura shogunate, founded by the victorious Minamoto Yoritomo in 1192, finally collapsed, and a new seat of military government was established in Kyoto under the shoguns of the Ashikaga family, a branch of the Minamoto. Though the fighting continued (rarely was there a peaceful interlude of more than ten or twenty years), the Ashikaga period was nevertheless outstanding for its artistic achievements and for establishing canons of aesthetic taste and judgement which were to endure. Unlike the art of the Heian period which flourished in a rarefied atmosphere of privilege and luxury, and was the prerogative of courtiers, that of the Ashikaga derived from a variety of sources. To the refinement of the imperial court was added the vigour and Zen disciplines of the samurai, the scholarship and artistry of Buddhist priests and philosophers, and the fruits of newly established official relations with China, now in the early years of the Ming dynasty.

Together with yugen, the qualities most sought after and admired were those of 'sabi' and 'wabi'. Sabi, literally 'rust', means the taking of pleasure in something which bears the marks of time, whilst wabi, literally 'poverty', denotes a taste for the simple and quiet. The Ashikaga shoguns, as is customary with those who achieve supreme power, did not hesitate to celebrate their exalted status in the graciousness of their living, but any tendency towards ostentation was now tempered by the requirements of sabi, wabi and yugen. Beside a small lake in the wooded hills above Kyoto, Shogun Yoshimitsu built, in 1397, his magnificent Golden Pavilion, the Kinkakuji, which is so elegantly proportioned and carefully sited that it succeeds in harmonizing with its natural surroundings in spite of the opulence of its gold covering. Nearly a century later, Shogun Yoshimasa crossed to the opposite side of the Kyoto valley to build his rival Silver Pavilion, the Ginkakuji, and place before it a starkly sculpted mound of sand, the focus of attention for guests invited to contemplate moonlight.

Such was the artistic sensibility of the age, and it was nowhere better demonstrated than in the tea ceremony. Tea had been introduced from China as long ago as the ninth century, and at the beginning of the medieval period had been used as medicine and as a stimulant to help the acolytes of Zen to stay awake during long hours of meditation. In the fourteenth century, it provided an excuse for exuberant parties, accompanied by communal bathing, gambling, and much drinking of sake, but gradually the influence of Zen increased, until it had transformed tea-taking into a semireligious ritual.

'Wabi-cha', the most refined and austere form of the tea ceremony, survives today as a most comprehensive and complete demonstration of medieval taste. The tea bowl itself should be of plain pottery, and possess the dignity and mellowness of age, 'sabi'. Other utensils should be of different materials and textures – a tea caddy of china, a whisk of split bamboo, a kettle of iron, an incense box of black lacquer, and care should be taken to avoid repetition in shape or colour. The tearoom, the 'Abode of Fancy' like the study chamber of a medieval Zen monastery, should be small and austerely free of decoration – only an alcove, the 'tokonoma', the equivalent of the Zen altar, may contain a splash of colour in the form of a work of painting or calligraphy, together with an arrangement of flowers carefully chosen for the occasion. The teahouse, constructed of unpainted wood and with a roof of thatch, should merge unobtrusively with its natural surroundings and should be approached by a garden path of irregularly laid stones to symbolize the first step towards enlightenment. In everything, the emphasis should be on 'refined poverty', on irregularity, asymmetry and incompleteness (which invite the imagination to complete the scene), on the total absence of ostentatious decoration and, above all, on harmony with nature. Within such surroundings, it was believed, there could be harmony among men.

In front of most Shinto shrines there is a stylized
gateway, the 'torii' or 'bird-perch'. At Miyajima, an
island close to Hiroshima, the largest torii in the
world stands offshore, in the waters of the Inland Sea.

Overleaf The island of Sakurajima faces the city of
Kagoshima across a narrow strait, and it is dominated
by the triple cone of an active volcano.

The seventeenth-century garden of the
Shugakuin Imperial Villa in Kyoto.

The small garden of a samurai house in Kyushu. The
Japanese landscape garden is an artificial composition
of rocks, trees, shrubs and running water, which seeks
to disguise its artificiality and create an impression of
natural harmony and tranquillity within a confined space.

Above An avenue of 3000 stone lanterns marks the
approach to the ancient Shinto shrine of Kasuga in Nara.

Opposite The tea ceremony had a profound influence on the
design of buildings and on the landscaping of the gardens
which surround them and, in Kyoto, the teahouses of the
Katsura Imperial Villa are fine examples of architecture
blending unobtrusively with the natural surroundings.

The Kasuga shrine was founded in 768 as the tutelary shrine of
the Fujiwara family, who were later to rise to pre-eminence among
the nobility of the Heian court. As in the case of the Grand Shrine
of Ise, it was the custom at Kasuga to reconstruct the shrine
buildings every 20 years in replica of the original architecture.

The Kinkakuji, Kyoto's Golden Pavilion, was built in 1394 by
Shogun Yoshimitsu and used as a monastic retreat in the years
of his retirement. In 1950 the pavilion was destroyed by arson,
but it was rebuilt five years later, an exact copy of the original.

The lavishly embellished towers and pavilions of the
Toshogu shrine on Mount Nikko mark the final resting place
of Shogun Tokugawa Ieyasu. They were built in 1636 by
Ieyasu's grandson, Shogun Iemitsu, using the labour of
15,000 men and 2,500,000 sheets of gold leaf for the gilding.

The Heian shrine in Kyoto was built in 1895 to
celebrate the 1100th anniversary of the founding of
the city. Its buildings are a replica, on a reduced
scale, of the first Imperial Palace, built in 794.

Farmland near Kyoto.

The luxurious refinement of the house of the Shimazu
daimyo accords with their status as Lords of Kagoshima
through nearly 700 years of the feudal age.

Kyoto's Sanjusangendo temple contains 1001 identical
images of the 'Thousand-Handed' Bodhisattva Kannon,
the Merciful One who 'surveys the world with pity'.

Lions and a group of Chinese philosophers form part
of the lavish decoration on the Yomeinon, the 'Gate of
Sunlight' at Nikko. The gate was built in 1636 as a
central feature of the Toshogu mausoleum, and it received
the attentions of the finest artists of the day.

Opposite Gold embroidery on a delicate silk kimono
of the early Edo period.

A statuette of Uzen, the inventor of a dyeing
process which greatly facilitated the design and
manufacture of kimonos in the Edo period.

Opposite The painter and calligrapher Sato Taikan.

Chin Jukan is the descendant of a family of potters who came
to Japan from Korea 400 years ago. In the main living room of his
home, he has assembled the work of his family through fourteen
generations. By the end of the sixteenth century, the tea ceremony
had drawn attention to the quality of craftsmanship in tea
bowls and other utensils, and it may have been for this reason
that the daimyo of Kagoshima, Shimazu Yoshihiro, returned from
the Korean campaign of 1597 with a group of potters as his
prisoners of war. Among them was the ancestor of Chin Jukan.

Window displays of plastic food. Whether it be real or
imitation, food in Japan is always arranged to please the eye.

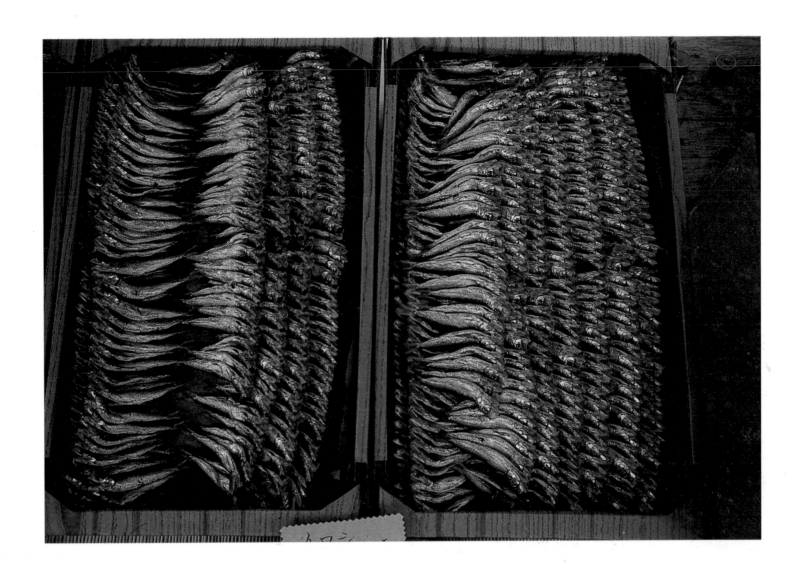

Fresh fish for sale in a shrine market.

Empty sake barrels in the Toshogu shrine at Nikko.
In Shinto, rice is regarded as sacred, a symbol of
the abundance of nature, and sake rice wine, like
rice itself, is a form of offering in Shinto ritual.

'Mikoshi', 'palanquins of the gods', stand on display
within the Yasaka shrine in Kyoto. In the Gion festival
they are carried to the Kamo river by teams of
young men, and purified by the sprinkling of holy water.

The Japanese love of patterns and groupings is apparent even in
the ostensibly haphazard display of this Kyoto antique shop.

Fireworks for sale in the Yasaka shrine during the Gion festival.

The Imperial Palace of Tokyo, the home of Emperor Hirohito,
stands on the site of Edo castle, and it is encircled by
a series of moats and high stone walls built by Shogun
Ieyasu at the beginning of the seventeenth century.

In Kyoto, the old Imperial Palace now stands empty,
but it continues to be maintained in immaculate
order as an impressive showpiece for visitors.

3
MUSIC OF A THOUSAND AUTUMNS

In returning to the roots of Japanese theatre, a deep love of nature is to be found which inspired poetry and painting. The first dances were offerings to the gods of nature, acts of worship performed in Shinto shrines, and so too were the magic antics of simple puppets, the distant relatives of today's bunraku. The solemn art of noh also began as a form of Shinto ritual, and its plays were performed in natural settings of great beauty. At Itsukushima shrine on the Inland Sea near Hiroshima, the noh stage was built by the edge of the shore, and, at high tide, appeared to float on the water.

The music of gagaku which accompanies the ancient dances is itself wonderfully evocative of nature. It has the ability to suggest the sound of wind sighing in the pines, the cracking-together of bamboo stalks in a thicket, the piercing cry of an owl, or the incessant buzzing of crickets, and at the Grand Shrine of Ise it is played in the open air, a hymn to the sun.

According to a popular story of Shinto mythology, Japanese theatre was created on a day when the world was plunged into darkness because the Sun Goddess had been angered by her brother, the God of Storms, and had hidden her light in a cave. To entice her out again, the Goddess of Happiness and Mirth performed a gaily erotic dance until her clothes fell off, thereby causing much amusement among the other gods gathered at the mouth of the cave. When the Sun Goddess looked out to discover the cause of the commotion, the world was bathed in sunlight once more.

There is nothing gay or erotic in the sacred dance 'Ninjo-mai' which re-enacts that famous event today. On the contrary, after nearly twenty centuries of refinement, it is solemn and stately, like the music which accompanies it, and this is perhaps appropriate for a dance which is probably the world's oldest.

Though gagaku, the 'Elegant Music of a Thousand Autumns', embraces the early dances of Shinto, its repertoire consists mainly of dances, 'bugaku', imported from China in the seventh and eighth centuries and preserved ever since by the Imperial Court. Performance of court dances was a matter of inherited privilege, and today many members of the Imperial Court Orchestra trace back their family line through twelve centuries of gagaku tradition, the oldest unbroken tradition of orchestral music and dance which exists anywhere in the world.

A close relation of bugaku was 'gigaku', imported from China in 612. Like bugaku, it made effective use of masks, though in a more light-hearted manner. By the early twelfth century, gigaku had given rise to 'sarugaku', 'monkey dances', which included a lot of clowning, conjuring tricks, puppetry and acrobatics, and provided interludes of light relief between ritualistic dances of 'spell-makers' in Shinto shrines and Buddhist temples. Gradually the sarugaku actors adopted elements of the competing entertainments – of magic ritual, of the stately dances of bugaku, and of folk dances, 'dengaku', which had been patronized by the court nobility and endowed with an air of sophistication. From this mixture, in the fourteenth and fifteenth centuries grew the form of theatre which came to be known as noh, 'the display of talent'.

The outstanding personality in the history of noh was Zeami, the most famous actor and playwright of his time. In 1374, Shogun Yoshimitsu attended a performance in which Zeami and his father Kan'ami were taking part. He was captivated by Kan'ami's acting and so taken by the physical charms of Zeami, then eleven years old (Yoshimitsu was seventeen), that he became their patron. Yoshimitsu lived up to his title 'Barbarian-conquering Great General', but he combined with his military skills the artistry of the courtier, being also a musician and a poet of repute. Under his patronage and personal guidance, the work of Zeami became increasingly subtle and sophisticated, and by the time of Yoshimitsu's death, sarugaku had been transformed from an earthy entertainment of 'monkey dances' into a theatre of refinement that was able to satisfy the most discerning tastes.

Like its contemporary, the tea ceremony, noh was much influenced by the meditative calm and mysticism of Zen, and it epitomized the artistic ideals of the late Middle Ages: 'bare, yet evocative, like the monochrome landscapes; beautiful, yet austere, like the temple gardens'(8). The actors walked with the dignity of the samurai and the decorum of the Zen priest, barely lifting their feet from the floor, and their aim was to capture the illusive and mysterious quality of yugen, the suggestion of profound meaning hidden behind worldly appearances.

Yugen lay at the very heart of the noh play, but it was a concept which, like Zen itself, defied exact definition:

If one is asked where yugen may be found in these sights, one cannot say; a man who cannot understand this truth is quite likely to prefer the sight of a moon shining brightly in a cloudless sky. It is quite impossible to explain wherein lies the interest or wonder of yugen.(8)

In his plays Zeami looked for the dramatic counterpart of the clouds and mist which, in concealing a landscape, lend it an air of mystery and stimulate the imagination. As guidance to his actors, he gave his idea of yugen with the phrase, 'In Silla at midnight the sun is bright'. To symbolize stillness he suggested 'Snow piled in a silver bowl', and in choosing the flying squirrel as the epitome of crudity and coarseness, he quotes Confucius: 'The flying squirrel has five talents. It can climb a tree, swim in the water, dig a hole, fly and run. But these five talents are appropriate to the level of the flying squirrel; it performs none of them well.'(8)

At the close of the medieval period, the noh play found a new patron in Hideyoshi, the general who had risen from the rank of foot soldier to become the unifier and undisputed ruler of all Japan. Like Yoshimitsu before him, Hideyoshi developed a passion for noh but, unlike his predecessor, he made use of the art to enhance his own prestige. Previously it had been the convention to set the plays in remote antiquity or, at the very latest, during the twelfth-century Gempei war. Hideyoshi ignored this convention and commissioned plays set in his own time, with himself as chief protagonist and hero. In a final manifestation of egomania, he even took to the stage and performed the central role himself before an audience of the court nobility. There could hardly have been a more radical break with noh tradition, and in celebrating recent events rather than those of bygone times, Hideyoshi was establishing a precedent for the highly topical kabuki and bunraku plays of the next century.

After the death of Hideyoshi, noh returned to its state of classical refinement as the official entertainment of the Tokugawa shoguns. Confucianism required music and ritual as necessary features of government, and noh was expected to supply this need.

At this time, actors were considered too base to be classified at all, but such was the status of noh that its most distinguished performers were ranked as samurai – somewhat of a mixed blessing, since a serious error in performance could lead to ritual disembowelment. The actors, like everyone else, were subject to a code of behaviour which encouraged modesty of living.

The noh play itself however was given an air of splendour, with costumes of the greatest magnificence. But the austere emptiness of the stage remained, and the ritual aspect of performance was emphasized at the expense of dramatic content. The transformation from public entertainment to high art was complete. Noh had become the exclusive property of the samurai élite and the people went off to seek their own diversion elsewhere – in the theatres of kabuki and bunraku.

Kabuki comes from the verb 'kabuku', meaning 'to deviate from the normal manners and customs, to do something absurd'. Today kabuki is performed only by men, but the first kabuki performance was given in about 1603 by a girl, a shrine maiden of Kyoto named O-Kuni, who 'deviated from the normal customs' by dressing as a man and entertaining the public with satirical dances in the grounds of the Kitano shrine.

O-Kuni's dances were so popular that prostitutes were often called upon to copy them; this led to a ban by the Tokugawa government on kabuki dances by women, and to the use of pretty young boy actors instead. This in turn 'stimulated the practice of sodomy, which had not been uncommon among the warriors and clergy, and now began to appeal to the townspeople as well'. Again the government took action, insisting that only adult male actors could perform kabuki, and thereby establishing the tradition of 'onnagata', male actors specializing in female roles.

As kabuki was developing from simple one-act sketches into a fully fledged theatrical entertainment, it had a powerful rival in the puppet theatre, then known as 'joruri'. Joruri was, in fact, the name of a girl who captured the heart of the hero Yoshitsune in the aftermath of the Gempei war, and their romance became a favourite theme of minstrels singing to the accompaniment of the Japanese lute, the 'biwa'. By the start of the seventeenth century, the biwa had been replaced by the 'samisen', a three-stringed plucked instrument with a strident tone, and the joruri songs of the minstrels had been combined with the puppets of sarugaku. Gradually the puppets became more expressive and sophisticated, and they attracted the attentions of the leading writers of the time. In particular, the work of Chikamatsu, the 'Shakespeare of Japan', was to endow the puppet literature with masterpieces of writing to rival anything in kabuki or noh. Chikamatsu actually preferred the puppet theatre to kabuki because the puppets told his stories with complete fidelity to the words he had written, whereas kabuki actors felt free to improvise at will, treating the script as no more than a vehicle for their own flights of fancy.

In 1703, Chikamatsu confirmed his reputation as the greatest of joruri playwrights with *Sonezaki Shinju*, 'The Love Suicides at Sonezaki', the story of a young merchant of soy sauce who commits joint suicide with the girl he loves, a prostitute. The play was based on an actual event which had taken place only a month earlier, and it caused a sensation. Instead of setting his play in the distant past and recounting the exploits of legendary heroes, Chikamatsu had chosen the present, and his characters were ordinary people much like the members of his audience. Now, for the first time, the people could come to the theatre, and see themselves and the predicaments which faced them in daily life, portrayed on stage by puppets seemingly endowed with human vitality and emotion.

The puppet theatre became enormously successful, and by the early eighteenth century its popularity far exceeded that of kabuki. Such was its importance that many puppet plays were adapted for kabuki, and the kabuki actors even took on some of the mannerisms of puppets. Consequently, the repertoires of kabuki and joruri – later named bunraku in honour of a famous puppeteer – became very similar.

Plays for bunraku usually provided the puppets with plenty of action and took advantage of their special talents for magical transformations, whilst those for kabuki were obliged to consider the whims and foibles of the actors themselves, and allow them scope for improvisation. But in both, the plots were very much the same, and there were familiar situations which arose again and again – severed heads were carried around in boxes, lovers committed suicide together as the only way out of impossible situations, and children were sacrificed in the cause of duty. Today, the plays offer a vivid portrait of life under the Tokugawa shoguns, and their recurring themes reveal an obsession with the tortuous demands of loyalties and obligations, and with ritual suicide as a means of regaining lost honour.

In 1748, the play *Chushingura*, 'The Treasury of Loyal Retainers' and popularly known as 'The Tale of the Forty-seven Ronin', was based on an extraordinary sequence of events which had taken place forty-five years earlier; it concerned a conflict of loyalties, of loyalty to one's lord with obedience to the law of the land. On a visit to the shogun's court, the provincial Lord Asano had offered to a high official Lord Kira, a gift which was deemed inadequate. In reply, Kira had tricked Asano into the humiliation of appearing at court incorrectly dressed, and Asano had reacted to this insult by drawing his sword and attacking the official, thereby sealing his own fate.

Asano was ordered to commit ritual suicide, seppuku, and his retainers became ronin, masterless samurai, with the duty to avenge their master's death. The ronin waited until Kira had relaxed his guard; then, on a snowy night in the middle of winter, they went to his home in Edo and, finding him hiding in a closet, killed him with the sword Asano had used for his own death a year earlier. They took Kira's head to lay at Asano's tomb, and surrendered to the authorities – in fulfilling their duties to their lord, they had broken the law and were therefore guilty of disloyalty to the emperor. It was a complicated situation, and at first the authorities could not decide what should be done, but after two months of uncertainty, the ronin were ordered to follow their master's example.

In writing their play, the authors of *Chushingura* were obliged to change the names of their characters and to place the action in the fourteenth century. This was in accordance with Tokugawa censorship which did not permit direct references to living, or recently living, members of the ruling élite. Nevertheless, everyone knew the truth of the matter, and the play was an immediate success. More than two centuries later, it stands as the greatest masterpiece of the mid-Edo period, and it is probably the most popular kabuki play of all.

After the end of the feudal period, kabuki and bunraku became set in their ways, their traditions jealously guarded by family hierarchies descended from the great actors and puppeteers of the eighteenth century. Playwrights were no longer attracted to the traditional stage but turned instead to more modern entertainments.

Today, there are new forms of theatre, which are much like those of the West; there is a thriving film industry; and as elsewhere, the most popular medium of entertainment is television. And yet, miraculously, the traditional theatre keeps going, and in some cases even shows signs of gaining strength. In his palace, the emperor still employs a gagaku orchestra of thirty musicians, though apparently he does not enjoy their music. The bunraku puppets of Osaka have lost none of their magic, in spite of falling attendances. Though its language is incomprehensible, noh continues to attract a small and select audience of connoisseurs whilst, in Tokyo, it is not uncommon to find the gigantic kabuki theatre of 2600 seats full to capacity. There, if they have time enough and patience enough, the people can escape from the grey and predictable world of the present to a romantic age of colour and fantasy, heroism and adventure.

Certainly kabuki today is the most spectacular form of the traditonal theatre and the most accessible. Its stage is enormous, its scenery is elaborate and capable of miraculous transformations, and its costumes, accurately reproduced for every period of Japanese history, are a delight to the eye. Though the eroticism and vivid bloodletting which were popular features of the original productions have now been refined almost out of existence, kabuki still has the power to startle and delight, to move its audience to tears at one moment, and to draw from them loud cries of approval at another.

Inside the noh theatre, the atmosphere is very different. The square stage is bare and empty. There is no scenery, except for a painted backdrop of a solitary pine tree. There may be no more than two actors, and in the course of the play very little will actually happen. The noh play makes considerable demands on its audience, but it has a power and a magic uniquely its own, and it is as limitless in its possibilities as the human imagination:

Out of the quiet repose of Noh rises an exultation. Once the spectator becomes geared to Noh's rhythms, each lift of the hand, each movement of the tightly stockinged foot, the opening and closing of a fan, the twirling of a long, rustling sleeve, assume immense meanings. Your mind rages with emotions.(9)

The Dance of White Herons is believed to have originated in
the ninth century as a feature of Shinto rituals to rid Kyoto of
disease. After proving successful, the rituals gave rise to the
annual Gion festival, and today the Heron dance is still
performed at the Yasaka shrine as part of the festival activities.

In the Gion festival, young girls finish their dance with a deep
bow of respect to their audience, and to the gods of the shrine.

At Kasuga Shrine in Nara, the shrine maidens, 'miko', perform
one of the sacred 'kagura' dances. Though the form of the
dance may be almost 2000 years old, the words of the musical
accompaniment were written by Emperor Hirohito only forty
years ago, and they express his wish for world peace.

Near the Grand Shrine of Ise, shrine maidens dance the ancient
'yamato mai', symbolizing the creation of Japan and the Japanese
people. They carry branches of the sacred 'sakaki' tree.

Opposite 'Genroku' is a bugaku dance which came from India via China
in the eighth century. It shows a snake-eater hunting for his food.

Bugaku has been preserved for 1200 years by courtiers of the
Imperial Palace, and it is normally performed exclusively
by men. These girls in Sagimori shrine in Kyoto are amateurs
who perform the old dances chiefly for their own amusement.

'Bairo' is a martial dance from China. In the seventh century,
it was performed before battle, and the quality of the music
was believed to indicate the likelihood of victory or defeat.

Opposite In the Imperial Palace in Tokyo, a bugaku dancer
performs 'ryo-o'. The dance is based on the legend of a Chinese
warrior, so handsome that he was obliged to use a fearsome
mask in battle in order to terrify his enemies.

The modern noh stage is a copy of a theatre built
in the grounds of Edo castle by one of the Tokugawa
shoguns, and it is covered by a symbolic temple roof.
The stage floor is made of highly polished cypress
wood and, beneath it, large earthenware jars act as
resonators to amplify the sound of stamping feet.
Opposite The sorrowful ghost of an old man in the
noh play *Koi-no-Omoni*. Masks are the very lifeblood
of noh, and they are treated with awe and
respect by the actors who wear them.

Though masks of spirits and demons often bear an expression
of startling intensity, noh masks for women are almost
expressionless, but are so designed that a small inclination
of the head will appear to produce a subtle change of mood
by catching the light at a slightly different angle.

In a kabuki play of the late Edo period, the lovers Izayoi
and Seishin decide on joint suicide so that they may
be reborn together to a new life.

Overleaf Izayoi and Seishin survive their suicide
attempt, but circumstances compel them to adopt a life
of crime. Eventually the police catch up with them, and
there is a violent struggle. As excitement mounts, suddenly
the action freezes, and the play comes to an end.

Terakoya, 'The Village School', one of kabuki's most
popular stories, was first presented in 1746 as a
puppet play. It tells of a retainer who proves his
loyalty to his former master by sacrificing his own
son, and in this final scene the retainer and his
wife wear mourning clothes of white and pale turquoise
as they prepare for the burial of their child.
Opposite The role of Izayoi, the courtesan turned crook,
is played by the actor Tamasaburo.
In kabuki, all female roles are played by male actors,
onnagata, and their mannerisms are so convincingly
feminine that even geisha come to see them, to learn
how a woman of distinction should dress and behave.

In contrast to the intimacy and spare simplicity of the noh
stage, that of kabuki is wide and spacious, with elaborate
constructions of scenery, rotating platforms, and trap doors
which will spring an actor into view as if by magic.

The actor Ennosuke plays the fox Tadanobu in the kabuki
story *Yoshitsune Senbon Zakura*. After his defeat of the Heike
clan in the twelfth-century Gempei war, Yoshitsune was
forced to flee from his jealous and suspicious brother,
Shogun Yoritomo, and he appears in many a play of the
classic theatre as a character at once heroic and tragic.
In this scene, a fox disguises itself as a retainer of Yoritomo
in order to be near a drum made from the hide of its parents.

On the small island of Sado, an old man and his puppets entertain the
fishermen with stories of heroism and adventure. Four hundred years
ago, it was puppet shows like this which gave birth to the sophisticated
theatre of bunraku, but the tradition is very much older. Nearly
1000 years ago, a Heian courtier wrote of nomadic companies of
puppeteers who made their living by hunting, and whose womenfolk enticed
travellers to sleep with them. They were described as resembling 'the
northern barbarians' and were probably immigrants from the Asia mainland.

Overleaf Puppet characters await their cue on the beach of Sado island.

The moment when a puppet appears on stage is often one of high drama,
and so convincing are the gestures that he seems to move of his
own accord, dragging his three operators behind him.
Previous pages The puppets of bunraku are considerably more elaborate than
folk puppets, especially those for male characters. With the assistance
of three operators they can move their eyes, raise their eyebrows, open
and shut their mouths, and turn their heads from side to side. The puppets
are a little larger than half life-size. Lady puppets have no need of
feet, since their kimonos reach to the ground, and their faces are less
expressive than those of the men. Usually they carry a look of sadness,
since the life of the bunraku heroine is rarely joyful but often tragic.

116

Bunraku is a theatre of stylized conventions and does not
aim at total realism. One is always aware that the puppets
are puppets and not human beings, and yet they appear to be
magically endowed with human vitality and emotion, and in this
apparent contradiction lies the true fascination of bunraku.

Just as the kabuki actor will mark a climactic moment
in the action by adopting a rigid pose, 'mie', with
an exaggerated facial expression, so in bunraku
a puppet may give vent to strong emotion with a
series of poses, 'kata', accompanied by raised eyebrows,
clenched fists, and a stamp of the foot.
Opposite Heroines are not permitted the open display of emotion, and
they hide their feelings with the help of a towel or a fold of their kimono.

4

THE PALACE OF THE DRAGON KING

Under the Tokugawa shoguns little more than a century ago, it was considered indecent for lovers to show affection in public, and until recently it was rare, even in Tokyo, to find a young couple walking hand in hand. In spite of kabuki's erotic overtones, love scenes in the theatre were, and still are, played with the greatest delicacy. The lady may perhaps demonstrate her affection by combing her lover's hair but, otherwise, heroes and heroines will rarely touch each other and certainly they will never kiss – when the celebrated actor Ennosuke tried to introduce the kiss to the kabuki theatre, there was a public outcry, and the whole thing was quickly forgotten. At the heart of this seemingly puritan behaviour lay the moral attitudes of Confucianism, with its narrow definitions of appropriate conduct for each individual in every conceivable situation. But it was a morality based on expediency rather than a religious one in the Christian sense, and Confucianism had no absolute objections to prostitution. In the words of Shogun Ieyasu himself: 'Strumpets, dancing-girls, sodomites, and street-walkers are people who will certainly be found in castle towns and prosperous places, and though they are the cause of bad conduct in many, yet if they are strictly prohibited very great evils will be continually arising.'(1)

Knowing that it would never be possible to eradicate prostitution altogether, the shoguns preferred to legalize and control it, just as they did everything else, and in the early 1600s, a citizen of Edo was given permission to establish a red-light district in return for passing secret information about those who used its facilities. He chose an empty field on the outskirts of the city, and there established the pleasure quarters of the Yoshiwara, 'the plain of reeds'. After a fire in 1656, the now-thriving Yoshiwara was moved to the vicinity of the Sensoji temple in the Asakusa district and there it remained for the next three hundred years.

The Sensoji temple was renowned for a small golden image which was thought to have miraculous powers, and pilgrims were drawn to it from all over the country. In their wake came a flood of merchants, entertainers and courtesans, anxious to serve their needs, and the Yoshiwara flourished. It became a city within a city, self-sufficient, and with every kind of urban amenity. At the peak of its career, it enjoyed a splendour which was 'by day like Paradise, and by night like the Palace of the Dragon King'. The Yoshiwara was a pleasure quarter, a 'Flower-and-Willow-World' of grandiose proportions and the haunt of actors, artists, musicians and writers, who drew inspiration from its colourful atmosphere and celebrated the charms of its courtesans in their work.

The Yoshiwara was the embodiment of 'ukiyo', the 'Floating World'. Originally, ukiyo had negative connotations, being used by Buddhists to describe the uncertainties and illusions of human existence, but in the seventeenth century it came to signify the virtues of a life of pleasure, 'a world in which one lives for the moment, gazing at the moon, snow, blossoms and autumn leaves, enjoying sake, women and song, and generally drifting with the current of life like a gourd floating downstream'. This was the world of the wood-block prints, 'ukiyo-e', which were produced in great quantities to satisfy public demand. Previously, the patrons of art had been the samurai, the courtiers and the priesthood, and paintings had been commissioned for the screens and walls of temples and castles. Now, the lower classes had an art form of their own, and one which was able to attract the finest artists of the time.

In the work of Hiroshige and Hokusai they could see themselves as they were in daily life, building houses, sawing wood, celebrating festivals, lifting and carrying, and travelling to and from Edo through a familiar landscape dominated by Mount Fuji. The prints of Sharaku immortalized the famous actors of kabuki in dramatic poses of startling intensity, whilst those of Utamaro featured the courtesans, languid and sensual, the élite of the Floating World. Many of the pictures were joyfully and blatantly pornographic, with an eroticism heightened by the enveloping folds of luxurious silk kimonos; and, perhaps through association with the fertility cults of Shinto, they were highly esteemed for their power to ward off evil spirits, and used as magical protection against fire.

In kabuki, as in prints and novels and the real Yoshiwara, the courtesan was the centre of attention, and she represented the ideals of feminine beauty and grace. Being available to anyone who could afford her price, she was of interest to samurai and townsfolk alike, and she became the subject of countless stories of romance and intrigue. The courtesan was no common prostitute. She was a lady of refinement, skilled in the courtly arts of music and dance and the writing of poetry, and often of good family. In kabuki plays, the courtesan is frequently the wife of a samurai, and she sells herself to a house of pleasure in order to give her husband the money to repay a debt and save the honour of his name. She is a person of strong moral fibre, capable of the supreme sacrifice, and it is usually she, rather than her lover, who makes the proposal of double suicide and ensures that it is carried out.

Though love suicides were quite frequent in real life, and actually increased in popularity as a result of their romantic portrayal on stage, the true heroism of the samurai wife lay in her obedience to the 'three-fold submission' demanded by Confucianism: submission to her husband's parents, to her husband, and to her adult male offspring.

Approach your husband as you would Heaven itself, for it is certain that if you offend him Heaven's punishment will be yours ... The great Life-long duty of a woman is obedience. In her dealings with her husband both the expression of her countenance and the style of her address should be courteous, humble, and conciliatory, never peevish and intractable, never rude and arrogant – that should be a woman's chiefest care ... Ever attentive to the requirements of her husband, she must fold his clothes and dust his rug, rear his children, wash what is dirty, be constantly in the midst of his household, and never go abroad but of necessity ... The five worst maladies that afflict the female mind are indocility, discontent, slander, jealousy and silliness. Without any doubt, these five maladies infest seven or eight out of every ten women, and it is from these that arise the inferiority of women to men.(3)

This interpretation of the Confucian code is contained in the treatise *Great Learning for Women*, attributed to Kaibara Ekken, a distinguished Confucian scholar of the late seventeenth century, and it formed part of the curriculum of the 'terakoya', the temple schools for the primary education of the common people, though it was originally written with the samurai in mind.

The life of a samurai wife was not one to be envied. Among the samurai there was no equivalent to the chivalry of the knights of medieval Europe, and apparently no room for romantic love, except that between one samurai and another. According to the social anthropologist Nakane Chie, the inferior–superior relationships considered ideal among samurai were so demanding that the men had 'little room left for a wife or sweetheart'; the emotions of a samurai were 'completely expended in his devotion to his master'.(10)

Though faithful to his lord, the samurai was not required to be sexually faithful to his wife. It was perfectly in order that he should visit courtesans, providing he took scrupulous care to avoid emotional entanglements – these would inevitably have provoked a conflict of 'giri', duty, with 'ninjo', human feelings. Consequently, the Yoshiwara was a melting-pot of every class and profession, where high-class courtesans and cheap prostitutes 'sold spring' to samurai, merchants and priests alike.

The Yoshiwara also bore the name 'Fuyajo', 'the city which knows no night'. It was encircled by a wall, and at midnight the gates were closed, thus obliging those trapped inside to continue their revelry until 6 a.m., when the gates would reopen. In accordance with the customary procedures of the shogunate, everything was classified and regulated, and there was a hierarchy of courtesans, graded according to age and accomplishments. They usually came to the Yoshiwara at the age of six or seven, having been sold to brothel owners by parents desperately in need of money. They began as apprentice prostitutes, and were instructed in dancing, singing, writing poetry, and the theory of lovemaking (though not as yet its practice). At twelve and seventeen they were examined in these subjects and if they passed with distinction they entered the highest category of courtesan, that of 'oiran'. This was itself subdivided into three grades, the highest of which was 'tayu'. In a census taken in 1689, the Yoshiwara was shown to employ nearly three thousand courtesans, but, of these, only three were in the top grade. The tayu were celebrities, the pride of Edo, and lavish gifts were showered on them by wealthy patrons competing for their costly favours. On one occasion, a dealer in rice is reported to have bought up all the eels in Edo so that his tayu should be the only lady to dine that day on the great delicacy.

After the mid-eighteenth century, the fortunes of the Yoshiwara gradually declined.

It received a temporary reprieve at the end of the Pacific war, when young GIs of the occupation forces provided employment for forty thousand girls, but in 1958 it was forced to close down altogether. Women's organizations, led by newly elected female members of parliament, succeeded, after a campaign lasting eleven years, in forcing through legislation to make prostitution illegal. But they left a loophole which still has not been closed – it became illegal for a girl to 'sell spring', but not for a man to buy it, and today the cities abound in 'love-hotels' and Turkish baths, where all the traditional services of the Yoshiwara are available and, by a technicality of the law, are perfectly legal.

The true embodiment of the Yoshiwara tradition nowadays is the 'geisha', the 'art person', and she is certainly legal though, in so far as her sexual favours may be bought, she may still be regarded as a courtesan of refinement. Geisha now begin life, not as seven-year-old apprentice prostitutes, but as sixteen- or seventeen-year-old 'maiko' or dancing girls, and their social status is high. When the directors of a mighty industrial conglomerate come together for a routine monthly meeting, they may well do so in a geisha-house, with maiko and geisha in attendance. The girls will join them at the meal table, pour their beer and sake, dismember their fish, listen sympathetically to their shoptalk, and entertain them with samisen music, songs and dances. When the meeting is over, the bill will be extremely high, and the level of erotic stimulation rather low. But the participants will have the satisfaction that they behaved as men of refinement and played their part in supporting a truly Japanese institution.

If the client of a geisha-house is attracted to one of the maiko, and if she accepts him, the days of her apprenticeship are over, and she becomes a fully fledged geisha. He may now sleep with her, but in return he must give her somewhere to live, and money enough to buy kimonos and keep her in the manner which geisha expect. She will consider herself under obligation to her patron and, theoretically, she should not sleep with another man unless she has his permission. However, so ruinous is the cost of keeping a geisha, that it has become possible for two or more men to become patrons of the same girl, and to take it in turns to enjoy her company. This compromise with tradition is a desperate attempt on the part of the geisha-houses to stay in business. There are few geisha left: in the Gion area of Kyoto – for centuries a geisha enclave – there are now only twenty-seven geisha and four maiko, and very soon there may be none at all. The maiko must endure the imprisonment of tight kimonos, must sleep motionlessly with her neck on a wooden pillow in order to preserve her elaborate coiffure, and she must forego the companionship of boyfriends and the lively music of discos in order to learn ancient dances and entertain ageing company presidents. Not surprisingly, few young girls volunteer for the job – if glamour is what they are looking for, they are more likely to become actresses or models, or dancers in night clubs.

The Floating World of the present day is bewildering to the Western visitor, and it abounds in contradictions. Prostitution is illegal, but in Turkish baths and 'love-hotels' it flourishes. *Playboy* magazine is censored, with the intimate details of pictures covered over, but on the super-fast trains which dash between Tokyo and Osaka, businessmen bury their heads in erotic comic books which contain the most lurid scenes of sexual sadomasochism. A sizeable proportion of the Japanese film industry is devoted to the production of pornography and it is often sickeningly violent, but there is never a pubic hair to be seen. In 'businessmen's hotels' (as distinct from those catering for tourists), each room has a television set with a coin-in-the-slot machine, and the guest with a large stack of coins may avail himself of three hours of blue movies imported from Germany, Sweden and the USA, but again there is a prudish horror of pudenda, and genital areas are invariably disguised by fuzzy blobs.

The peddling of pornography is now a major industry, but it takes place in an atmosphere of moral confusion, and it seems Western influence is much to blame for this. In the past, the Shinto religion endowed the people with a healthily matter-of-fact attitude to the human body, to nudity and to sex. In celebrating the abundance of nature and the innate goodness and divinity of mankind, it made no connection between sin and sex, and the Shinto myth of creation is delightfully simple and straightforward:

'How is your body formed?' Izanagi asked his spouse, Isanami. 'My body', she replied, 'formed though it be formed, has one place which is formed insufficiently.'

'But my body,' continued Izanagi, 'formed though it be formed, has one place which is formed to excess. Therefore, I would like to take that place in my body which is formed to excess, and insert it into that place in your body which is formed insufficiently, and thus give birth to the land.'(4)

Confucianism, in the Edo period (1603–1868), sought to define the situations where sex was appropriate, and the Tokugawa administration, ever concerned for the morals of its samurai, attempted to suppress pornographic literature. Nevertheless, the Confucian code never suggested anything harmful in sex or nudity as such, and men and women continued to bath together in hot springs and public bathhouses without a shadow of embarrassment.

When the country opened its doors to the West, the innocence in sexual matters began to disappear. European visitors were clearly shocked by what they considered to be primitive and barbaric behaviour, and the Japanese Government hastily sought to restrict those practices – mixed bathing, tattooing, the sale of pornography – which the foreigners found most offensive. But, as often happens, censorship had the reverse effect of that intended – now that the female body was hidden from view, it became an object of sexual curiosity, and all the more desirable for being forbidden fruit. The demand for pornography increased greatly, and ingenious means were devised to make it available, in spite of the legal restrictions.

In Tokyo today, a prudery worthy of the Victorians lives side-by-side with the most blatant sexual exploitation. In the streets, young girls who would never dream of bearing their breasts in public appear not to notice the lurid posters advertising sadomasochistic films. Not a hundred yards from the kabuki theatre where the kiss is considered indecent, there is a complex of cinemas specializing in European pornography. On television, sex orgies are intermingled with serious political reporting, and nobody regards it as strange. In the Ginza and other high-class entertainment areas, nearly a hundred thousand girls are employed as hostesses for businessmen on generous expense accounts. The girls are attractive, they are dressed to kill, but they are not sexually available – the whole thing is an expensive tease, and thoroughly respectable. At 11 p.m. the Ginza closes down, the businessmen climb into their company limousines, and the hostesses go home to their families.

Little now remains of the spirit of the Yoshiwara, 'the Nightless City', but in Asakusa, in narrow streets lined with 'sutorippu' (strip) parlours and 'toruko-buro' (Turkish baths), there are bars where the Edokko – the cockneys of Tokyo – still gather late at night in the company of kabuki actors, film directors, fashion designers, and the occasional poet. In Japan, it seems, there is always someone to ensure that old traditions never die.

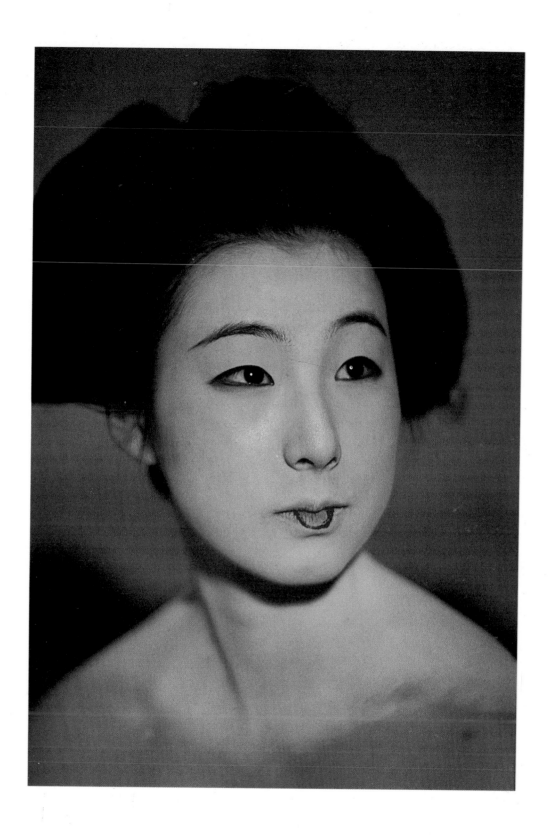

Someiyu is sixteen years old and a maiko, a geisha in the making. Geisha means 'art person', and for years she will study music and dancing, flower arrangement and calligraphy, and the art of polite conversation, and she will spend her evenings entertaining the clients of the geisha house which employs her.

Beside the kabuki theatre in Kyoto, Someiyu helps
the police by distributing anticrime leaflets.

Maiko may be distinguished from geisha by their more
elaborate hairstyles and more luxurious kimonos.

Yasaka shrine, founded in 876, is dedicated to Susano-
o-no-Mikoto, God of Storms and Tempests, and for centuries
it has been the favourite shrine of Kyoto courtesans.

Wigs are required for special geisha dances performed
during the Gion festival. Maiko and geisha always do
their own make-up. In whitening their already pale skins
they accentuate the lines of eyes and mouth, and provide
a neutral accompaniment to the strong colours of their kimonos.

After finishing her make-up Someiyu has been tightly bound into her
kimono, and she is ready for the first appointment of the evening.
Opposite Though wigs are used on special occasions, maiko and
geisha usually wear an elaborate coiffure of their own hair. Once
a week it is conjured into a shape known as 'split peach', and when
they sleep, the girls are obliged to rest their necks on wooden
pillows in order not to disturb the composition.

Geisha dances are most often seen as solo performances in
teahouses and exclusive restaurants, but in springtime
the geisha of Kyoto put on spectacular stage shows for the
public and perform their own versions of the kabuki classics.

Maiko Someiyu stands at the door of a geisha house in the Gion district
of Kyoto. For the pleasure of her company at the dinner table, the
client waiting inside will pay nearly £100, but he is unlikely ever to
see the bill – that will be sent discreetly to his company's accountant.

In contrast to the mysteriously anonymous façades of
geisha houses, the Love Hotels of Lake Biwa brashly
proclaim their role as palaces of pleasure, and they
constitute a small township of up-market bordellos.

One of the Biwa Love Hotels takes the form of a
medieval castle. 'Honoured guests' are received in
elegant surroundings of tatami matting and rice-paper
walls, and the girls are dressed in kimonos of blue silk.

In Tokyo today, the notorious red-light district of the
Yoshiwara no longer exists, but in the entertainment areas
of the city – Asakusa, Ginza and Shinjuku – there are many
thousands of bars with attractive hostesses, and nightclubs
offering sophisticated European-style striptease (*overleaf*).

Gangsters, 'yakuza', on their way to a village bathhouse.

Opposite A gangster boss with his champion fighting dog.

Japan has the lowest crime rate in the world, and the yakuza have little
in common with Al Capone. They control the Love Hotels, organize
dogfighting, and have been known to operate protection rackets;
but in general, their activities are not blatantly illegal, and they
make little attempt to disguise their identities. On the contrary,
they tend to emphasize their gangsterish ways with an arrogant
swagger, 'ibaru', the gruffness, 'aragoto', used in kabuki theatre
for fierce characters, and with bodies covered in tattoo.

In Japan people are powerfully aware of their obligations and loyalties to the various groups to which they belong – their family, their friends, their golfing companions, their workmates. Since a gang is a particularly well-defined group, gang society shows, in an exaggerated form, the feeling for hierarchy which is inherent in Japanese society. Among the yakuza there is an accepted pecking order, apparent even in a public bathhouse. There is also a strict code of honour and loyalty: disloyal conduct no longer leads to ritual disembowelment as it did among the samurai, but it will certainly lose a man a finger or two.

Opposite This man's tattoo shows a carp, a popular symbol of vigour and energy, 'ikioi', which comes from its ability to swim against the current and leap waterfalls.

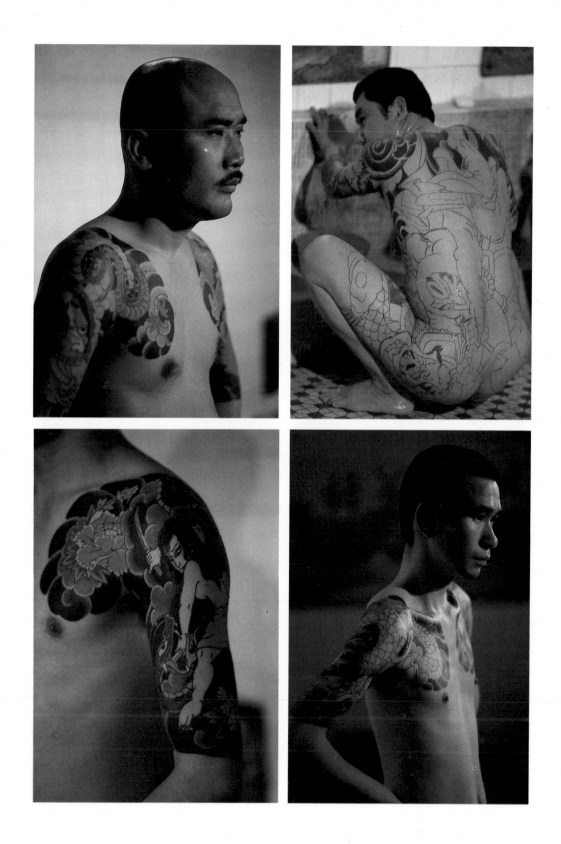

In choosing the themes of their tattoos, the
yakuza look to the past for inspiring ideals of
heroism and romance, and their bodies are a
veritable showcase of Japanese mythology.

5

JAPAN, THE CHILDREN'S PARADISE

In Japan, children below the age of five are, without embarrassment, openly treasured and admired, and given almost total freedom. It is as if their parents, who are themselves so tightly enmeshed by the web of etiquette and formal behaviour, can find through their children a feeling of release from the inhibitions of daily life. Young children have no 'meishi', business cards, to advertise their function and status. They have not yet learned to bow low to their superiors and do not yet understand the subtleties of high and low forms of speech, of 'respect language', which must be handled with care if no offence is to be given. They are free, and for a few precious years they are encouraged to enjoy their freedom to the full. 'Children know no shame', say the Japanese. 'That is why they are so happy!'

The word 'shame' is vastly more important in Japan than in the West. From the anthropological viewpoint Japan's is a 'shame culture', and good behaviour comes from the wish to avoid public ridicule and humiliation, and not from the urgings of a moral conscience as in the so-called 'guilt cultures' of Western countries. The Shinto religion has no equivalent to the Confessional of the Christian Church, and a Japanese who fails in fulfilling his social duties does not expect to be punished in the afterlife. For him, the ultimate punishment is social rejection, and in everything he sets out to win the approval and respect of those around him.

Towards the end of the Pacific war, the cultural anthropologist Ruth Benedict was asked to make a study of the Japanese character so that the Americans should better understand the enemy they were fighting. The results of her work were first published in 1946 in her book *The Chrysanthemum and the Sword*, and although she has been criticized for allowing value judgements to creep into an ostensibly objective analysis, the book has become a classic, highly recommended for its sympathetic account of Japanese thought and behaviour. She begins by pointing out that

the Japanese have been described by the most fantastic series of 'but also's' ever used for any nation of the world. When a serious observer is writing about peoples other than the Japanese and says they are unprecedentedly polite, he is not likely to add, 'but also insolent and overbearing'. When he says people of some nations are incomparably rigid in their behaviour, he does not add, 'But also they adapt themselves readily to extreme innovations' ... When he says they are loyal and generous, he does not declare, 'But also treacherous and spiteful' ... When he describes robot-like disciplines in their Army, he does not continue by describing the way the soldiers in that Army take the bit between their teeth even to the point of insubordination ... When he writes a book on a nation with a popular cult of aestheticism which gives high honour to actors and to artists and lavishes art upon the cultivation of chrysanthemums, that book does not ordinarily have to be supplemented by another which is devoted to the cult of the sword and the top prestige of the warrior ... The Japanese are, to the highest degree, both aggressive and unaggressive, both militaristic and aesthetic, both insolent and polite, rigid and adaptable, submissive and resentful of being pushed around, loyal and treacherous, brave and timid, conservative and hospitable to new ways.(11)

There have been many attempts to account for the dualism in the Japanese character, by foreigners and Japanese alike. The psychoanalyst Doi Takeo draws attention to 'amae', the desire of an infant passively to be loved and protected by its mother from the world at large. Dr Doi suggests that this desire is carried through childhood into adult life, and that much, if not most, of Japanese social behaviour may be understood as deriving from this one basic emotion. It explains, for example, the reliance on the warm, motherlike embrace of the group, the fear of conflict within the group, and the apparently childish behaviour of an adult who seeks the indulgence of another. In so far as the group shelters the individual from the realities of the world at large, it tends to promote a lack of objectivity, and behaviour which is intuitive rather than logical. Within his group, the individual will act with the greatest deference to his companions. Outside it, the more aggressive aspect of his personality may make itself felt.

The Australian writer Murray Sayle, now a resident of Tokyo, has a simpler and less sympathetic explanation to offer:

The Japanese have two standards: the impossible Samurai Code of courage and devotion to duty, heightened by centuries of romantic drama and literature to a level no mortal man could aspire to (although some of the Kamikaze pilots did their best), and the sly, looking-after-number-one, all-too-human business ethics of the Japanese merchants, the world of Japan's sordid political corruption and tricky trade policies. Both are very much alive, and often in the same man.(12)

In her own interpretation, Ruth Benedict has much in common with Dr Doi, and she also looks to the early years of life for the roots of adult behaviour:

The contradictions which all Westerners have described in Japanese character are intelligible from their child rearing. It produces a duality in their outlook on life, neither side of which can be ignored. From their experience of privilege and psychological ease in babyhood they retain through all the disciplines of later life the memory of an easier life when they 'did not know shame'. They do not have to paint a Heaven in the future; they have it in their past. They rephrase their childhood in the doctrine of the innate goodness of man, of the benevolence of their gods, and of the incomparable desirability of being a Japanese.(11)

Ruth Benedict continues by describing how the young child, from the age of six onwards, is led from freedom towards the constraints of adult life and an awareness of shame. The aggressiveness which a young boy has previously been allowed to indulge openly, even against his mother, is channelled into socially acceptable forms. His ego is restrained, and he is made ever more aware of his obligations, both within the family circle and outside it. A small mistake on his part may be used by his parents as an excuse to turn against him, on the grounds that he has brought disgrace on his family. When this happens, he cannot run to his peers for support and he is isolated. In Japan, where group activity is the norm, the individual receives support from his group only if his behaviour is beyond reproach, and this holds true even among children. From the bitter experience of rejection the boy comes to appreciate his responsibilities to those around him, and the importance of sublimating his own desires in the interests of whichever group they may appear to threaten – family, friends, school, neighbourhood, the country as a whole.

The sheer complexity of the laws governing Japanese social behaviour is awesome, and it is hardly surprising that they have offered rich source material for countless kabuki plays about the conflict between giri, duty, and ninjo, human feelings. An obligation is called 'on', and it is a debt passively incurred. From the very fact of being alive, one has a debt to parents, 'oya on'. In the course of life, other debts will be incurred: to one's teacher, 'shi no on', to one's lord, 'nushi no on' (nowadays this would apply to one's employer), and to anyone who may bestow a favour. The repayment of debts is a matter of the greatest importance, and it lies at the heart of social interactions. 'Gimu' is a term embracing debts which can never be fully repaid – loyalty to parents and ancestors and to one's place of employment, 'nimmu'. Debts which must be repaid with mathematical equivalence to the favours received, and within a specified time limit, come under the category of giri, and of these there are two kinds: 'giri-to-the-world', which includes specific duties to employers, relations, etc., and 'giri-to-one's-name', which implies the duty of clearing one's name of insult, of observing respect behaviour and, generally, of living according to one's station in life.

The observance of giri and gimu ensures the smooth running of the hierarchical society, where everyone knows his place and behaves accordingly. The child must be given an understanding of all this, and know when to bow, when to kneel, and which words to use when meeting people above or below in the social scale.

Every time a man says to another 'Eat' or 'Sit down' he uses different words if he is addressing someone familiarly or is speaking to an inferior or to a superior. There is a different 'you' that must be used in each case and the verbs have different stems. The Japanese have, in other words, what is called a 'respect language', as many other people do in the Pacific, and they accompany it with proper bows and kneelings. All such behaviour is governed by meticulous rules and conventions; it is not merely necessary to know to whom one bows but it is necessary to know how much one bows ... bows range all the way from kneeling with forehead lowered to the hands placed flat upon the floor, to the mere inclination of head and shoulders. One must learn early, how to suit the obeisance to each particular case.(11)

Though he lives in an increasingly Western-looking environment, the young

Japanese grows up in a cultural climate which is not Western at all, and he is constantly reminded of the past by being taken on group outings to ancient palaces and castles, sketchbook in hand. He will also participate in the festivals of shrines and temples which, in Japan, are still an essential feature of daily life. No great festival is complete without its parade of children immaculately decked out as samurai or princes, and they play their part with the utmost dignity and seriousness. Bravely they face the crowds and the banks of television cameras in solemn rituals of purification and in endless processions atop floats and palanquins, with never the flicker of a smile or any other show of emotion. Few responsibilities can be more burdensome to a Japanese child than those he may be called upon to bear at festival time – on him rests parental pride and the honour of the family name, and he makes sure that his behaviour is beyond reproach.

The same motivation of 'giri-to-the-world' underlies the apparent thirst for knowledge which has given Japan the highest literacy rate in Asia. At their studies, as in all else, the Japanese work with single-minded concentration and prodigious energy, but places in prestigious universities are limited and the ambitious student of today is caught up in a competitive rat race unparalleled throughout the world. Education in Japan has a long history; there were schools as far back as the fifteenth century. With the end of the Tokugawa regime in 1868, came important educational reforms and a system comprising elementary school, middle school and university, which formed the basis of modern education. As Japan opened her doors to the world at large, there was a passion among the people for things Western. In reaction against this, the government placed strong emphasis on traditional Japanese values, and the famous *Rescript on Education*, promulgated by the emperor in 1890, urged the young people to observe their Confucian obligations of filial piety, obedience and benevolence, and to offer themselves 'courageously to the state' should emergency arise. Every school had a copy of the rescript, and its importance in preparing young Japanese for the role they were to play in two world wars must have been considerable. Before he left on his suicide mission in late 1944, a twenty-three-year-old kamikaze pilot wrote to his father: '. . . the living embodiment of all wonderful things out of our past is the Imperial Family, which, too, is the crystallization of the splendour and beauty of Japan and its people. It is an honour to be able to give my life in defence of these beautiful and lofty things.'(13)

At the end of the war, one of the first acts of the occupying forces was to withdraw the rescript, and to make sweeping changes in the structure of education as a whole. The outcome was a coeducational system based on that of the USA, with kindergarten, elementary schools, lower and higher secondary schools, and universities distributed throughout the country. The new system was democratic, based on the concept of equal opportunity for all, but there remains to this day a clearly defined hierarchy where prestige is concerned. At the pinnacle stands Tokyo University, the traditional training ground of political leaders, but the student who fails to gain a place there still has other universities and colleges to try. It seems a large choice, and yet, so great is the demand, and so important the status of belonging to one of the more prestigious institutions, that the pressure on students is frightening. When their state schools fail to equip them for success they crowd into private cramming schools with classes of a hundred at a time, in a desperate attempt to win distinction for themselves and avoid the disgrace to the family name which comes with failure. For many the strain is too great, and the suicide rate among students today is alarmingly high. In the West, academic failure is felt as a personal disappointment, but in Japan it is a matter of shame and dishonour and, clearly, far more difficult to bear.

The whole of Japanese education seems aimed at equipping the student to function within the traditional social structure of hierarchies and groups, and in this it is strikingly different from the Western system which it was designed to emulate. Nowhere is this better demonstrated than within the universities. It is there that students in the West are encouraged to develop their individual personalities and aptitudes through intimate tutorials, private study and public debate. Japanese universities, on the other hand, concentrate on teaching identifiable attitudes to large numbers of students at a time, and conflicts of opinion tend to be avoided. Their gain over the West is in producing a disciplined and single-minded workforce which will never question authority, and which will devote the maximum effort to any task it may be given – an important contributing factor towards the extraordinary success of Japanese industry. Their loss is in the stifling of talent, imagination and flexibility of mind. It is not a system likely to produce great innovators – those who are capable of an inspired 'intuitive leap' – and it is not surprising that Japanese technology is distinguished by its ability to adopt, develop and produce, rather than by its originality and invention.

Neither is Japanese education likely to encourage artistic ability, in the sense that we know it in the West. The great individual talents, such as those of the writer Mishima and the film maker Kurosawa, came to fruition in defiance of social pressures urging them towards conformity, and even today they are more respected in the West than in their homeland. Art in Japan is more a matter of following the rules than of individual expression which comes from knowing when and how to break them and, as in Asia as a whole, a student rarely presumes to disagree with his 'sensei', his master, as he would be encouraged to do in Europe and America. Certainly, Japanese universities have had their share of unrest and, in the late 1960s, Tokyo University was set on fire during a violent student rebellion. But, like all else, it was a group activity and before long the same students were back at their lectures as if nothing had happened.

It is extraordinary that so few of the underlying values of Western education have taken root in Japan, but there is today one man at least who recognizes the need to develop qualities of individuality and leadership among young people. He is Matsushita Konosuke, now in his mid-eighties, founder and retired president of the giant Matsushita Electric Industrial Company, the makers of Technics Hi Fi and National Panasonic television sets amongst many other things. Mr Matsushita sees Japan as the leader of the world in the next century, and he has recently founded a school to train a hand-selected élite of young men in readiness for that time. His school is unique in Japan, in that it encourages its students to act as individuals, and Mr Matsushita, who, sixty-two years ago, had the courage to break away from the established company life and 'go it alone', is himself an inspiration to his protégés. It is an interesting experiment but unlikely to affect Japanese education as a whole, and perhaps the Japanese have little cause to hope that it should. In so far as their educational system accurately reflects the standards of society as a whole, and efficiently prepares its students for a life of selfless devotion to duty, it is, from a Japanese standpoint, ideal. As for the leaders of the future, they will be, like Mr Matsushita and Shogun Ieyasu before him, born, not made.

A young boy dressed as a courtier of the Heian period prepares
to ride through the streets of Kyoto in the Gion festival.

Overleaf At the Yasaka Shrine in Kyoto, children dressed
for Shinto dances pose for a photographer. In Japan the
group is more important than the individual, and no
occasion is complete without its group photograph.

In readiness for a festival procession, this young girl
has the white face which signifies purity and gentleness
of birth. Her companion wears a wig the colour of bravery
and passion, but it also suggests the attributes of a demon.

In the festival procession the boys are shielded from the
sun by the paper parasols of their attendants. The festival
day is 17 July, often the hottest of the year.

Pageboys of the Gion festival pose with their fathers
after a ceremony of purification in the Yasaka shrine.

Four days before the climax of the festival, the 'chigo', the pageboy of the god to whom the festival is dedicated, is dressed in the silk robes of a Heian nobleman and taken on a white horse, the 'horse of the gods', to a solemn ceremony of exorcism and purification in the Yasaka shrine.

Opposite The chigo is the figure of greatest importance in the Gion festival. Prior to the Edo period the chigo was always the son of a samurai, but on this particular occasion he is the son of a well-known samurai actor, Ikawa Hashizo.

The main event of the Gion festival is a procession of giant floats,
the 'hoko', and the chigo rides in the first of these, the Halberd
float. To start the procession he must use a sword to sever a sacred
rope of rice straw which is strung across the road in front of him.

In the 'Parade of a Thousand' at Nikko, the procession is led by
a group of boys in the resplendent silk robes of courtiers. They
play their part with dignity, and their impassive faces already
show the burden of tradition which will rule their lives.

In contrast to the magnificence of the festivals
in Nikko and Kyoto, that of Kaseda shrine in Kyushu
is a small village festival in which nearly everyone
participates. In feudal times Kyushu was notable for
the power of its great daimyo families, and in their
festival the villagers recall the heyday of the samurai
in vigorous dances and displays of martial art.

The Kaseda shrine, like many other shrines of Shinto, employs shrine maidens whose task it is to welcome visitors, supervise offerings, and perform sacred dances for the kami, the Shinto gods.

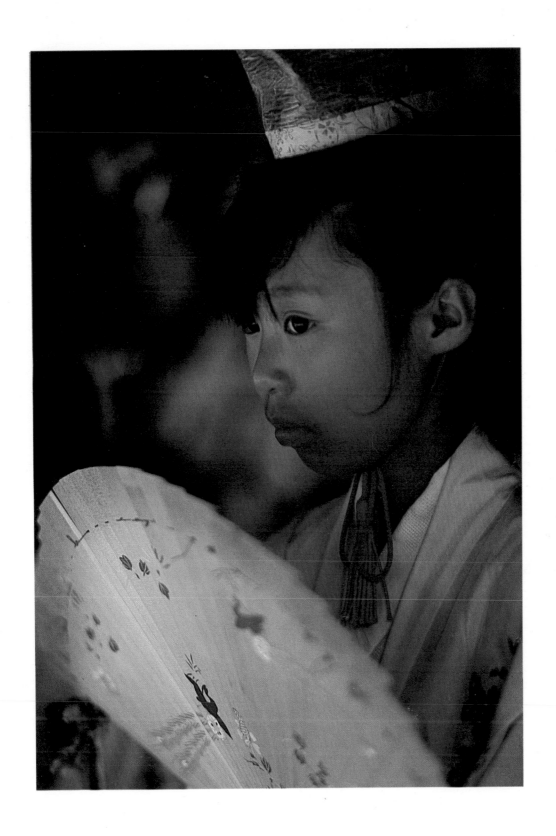

The Japanese people take a great delight in young children
and encourage their extrovert behaviour and spontaneity.
Nowhere is this better demonstrated than in the festivals of
shrines and temples where children are always much in evidence.

Above A young boy actor, the 'koyaku', takes the role of the
child emperor Antoku in a kabuki play about the twelfth-
century Gempei war. In kabuki, as in the more ancient
noh theatre, child actors are normally the real or
adopted sons of established company players, and
they make their stage début at about the age of five.

6

ECHOES OF A WARRIOR'S DREAM

Japan has recently been described as 'a spiritual abyss'(7), a nation 'squirming with cultural indigestion'(12) its people 'uncertain of their moorings in the cultural gulf that still separates East and West'. 'Tokyo is heartbreakingly, inexpressibly ugly . . . nothing to look at but concrete walls, tin roofs, neon signs, a jungle of criss-crossed electric wires . . . a monstrously overcrowded, jerry-built city, featureless as an ant heap'(12). Foreign visitors expecting to find the exotically beautiful world of picture postcards and wood-block prints recoil from the drab monotony of the industrial landscape, and the artificiality of plastic food and plastic flowers. What, they ask, has happened to that exquisite visual sense, that delight in simplicity and refinement which the world has come to regard as quintessentially Japanese? How could a people with a love of nature and obsession with purity consent to live in cities devoid of greenery and plagued by photochemical smog?

The usual answer to these questions is that the country is in thrall to industrial technology and, after a hundred years of exposure to Western influence, the Japanese are suffering from severe cultural schizophrenia, their native taste and judgement being in perpetual conflict with ideas imported from the West. In his life and his death, the writer Yukio Mishima appeared to support this interpretation. He

smoked American cigarettes, drank French brandy, entertained in Japanese formal dress in his Spanish-style house around his fake Louis XV dining table, wrote noh plays, acted in gangster melodramas, and finally killed himself (none too expertly) by ritual harakiri with a Japanese sword, after leading a comic-opera attempt at a military coup d'état.(12)

But it is possible that the true impact of Western culture has been much exaggerated. Before he died, Mishima called for the rejection of Western-style democracy and a return to the disciplines of the feudal age, but his words fell on deaf ears. His audience probably regarded him as a crazy fanatic, and thought his cause absurd. The situation was not half as bad as he supposed, and in fact the 'Japanese Spirit' was still very much alive. Westernization was really no more than a veneer, and beneath the surface it was still the innately Japanese attitudes of mind, not the Western ones, which determined the course of events.

When, at the end of the nineteenth century, Japan set out on the road to modernization, the watchword was 'wakon-yosai', 'Japanese Spirit with Western Technology'. In 1873, a large group of government leaders returned from an extensive tour of Europe and the USA and, partly as a result of their experiences, Japan was given a constitution based on that of Bismarck's Germany, an army trained by French instructors, and a navy modelled on that of Great Britain. From Italy, painters and sculptors were invited to Japan to reveal the secrets of European art, and the material culture of the West was adopted with enthusiasm – Japanese men exchanged their kimonos for Western-style suits and hats, carried rolled umbrellas, grew their hair, and learned to eat meat. At first it seemed as though Western spiritual values would also prevail but, in 1890, a backlash of nationalist feeling produced the imperial Rescript on Education, re-emphasizing the time-honoured traditions of Shinto and Confucianism, and ensuring the survival of wakonyosai, at least for the time being.

After the crushing defeat of the Second World War, the Japanese experienced a severe crisis of confidence in their native culture, and the institutions of Emperor-worship and bushido, the Way of the Warrior, which had been used to legitimize that disastrous military adventure, were discredited. This was to be expected, but few people among the occupying forces were prepared for the admiration, and total lack of resentment, which greeted them. The Japanese, it seems, have always been impressed by a show of strength, and they have the eminently practical ability to shift their allegiance to the winning side, providing they can do so with honour. This characteristic appears to derive from the realism of Shinto – an acceptance of the natural order of things leads to an ability to face facts. Having lost the war, they were quick to place their trust in General MacArthur, the blue-eyed shogun who had become their new ruler, and they set about the task of rebuilding their shattered land with grim determination.

Tokyo had been almost completely destroyed, and the speed of its reconstruction may account for much of the chaotic ugliness of the city today. Kyoto was spared the bombing in order to preserve its 'universal' heritage of temples and palaces, but it too has fallen prey to dehumanizing modernization, and has its share of concrete misery. The imperatives of rapid industrial expansion must have allowed little room for environmental considerations, but there may also be truth in the suggestion that the unwelcoming greyness of their cities derives, somewhat paradoxically, from the Japanese love of nature – the city is anti-nature, and so does not fall within the realm of aesthetic judgement. In their cities the Japanese do not even notice the ugliness of their surroundings, and therefore do not find them depressing.

The foreign visitor, who can never know how it must feel to be Japanese, should perhaps be cautious in his criticisms, but he can hardly fail to be dismayed by the quality of life he encounters in a modern Japanese city. The people appear to be suffering from compulsive neurosis, working to the limit in fear that otherwise people will think badly of them. They seem never to relax, except perhaps when soaking in a hot bath, and they spend most of their 'leisure' time mindlessly banging golf balls into nets, and flicking the levers of pinball machines in 'Pachinko' parlours. They are hidebound by convention, obsessed with hygiene, constantly in need of reassurance, and unable to take a decision unless it has been agreed by a sizeable committee.

Inevitably, from a Western point of view the Japanese way of life leaves much to be desired, but the fact remains that, for the Japanese, it works. Their cities function as cities should, their factories are the most highly productive in the world and the least plagued by strikes, they appear to enjoy their work and rarely complain, their crime rate is phenomenally low, and they do not appear to be seriously prone to mental illness. Though they live crowded together in tiny houses, and most people are obliged to spend three or four hours every day commuting, their faces show none of the strain and tension which one so often finds in the great cities of Europe and America.

In Tokyo there is energy and ebullience and a contagious enthusiasm. The city certainly does not convey the impression of conflict between the values of East and West – rather, it suggests a natural and happy continuity of established social patterns, with Westernization providing no more than a superficial gloss – in short, 'Japanese Spirit with Western Technology'.

The postwar recovery was little less than miraculous, a triumph of skill and determination, but the Japanese were fortunate in having inherited a pragmatic open-mindedness towards new ideas, together with a traditional social structure admirably suited to the needs of trade and commerce. As the social anthropologist Nakane Chie explains in her book *Japanese Society*, modernization was achieved 'not by changing the traditional structure, but by utilizing it'(10), and Japanese industry was built on foundations firmly laid in the days of Shoguns Ieyasu and Iemitsu. From Confucianism came the natural respect for authority which is so characteristic of the Japanese today – a most useful asset when it comes to organizing manpower. The need for an efficient and unquestioned chain of command was easily met by Confucian principles of hierarchy, and the ritual exchange of business cards ensured that everyone would be treated as befitted his professional status. Perhaps most important of all, the Confucian concept of filial piety encouraged the workers to place the interests of the company ahead of their own, and devote themselves unsparingly to their honourable duty – increasing production.

Twenty years ago, in the factories of the Matsushita Company in Osaka, the workers began the day by singing the company song:

> For the building of a new Japan
> Let's put our strength and mind together
> Doing our best to promote production,
> Sending our goods to the people of the world,
> Endlessly and continuously,
> Like water gushing from a fountain.
> Grow industry, grow, grow, grow!
> Harmony and sincerity!(4)

Today the company has achieved its aim, having become the largest manufacturer of television sets in the world. The workers still sing the company song, but the words have been changed:

A bright heart overflowing
With life linked together,
MATSUSHITA DENKI.
Time goes by but as it moves along
Each day brings a new spring.
Let us bind together
A world of blooming flowers
And a verdant land
In Love, Light and a Dream.

The emphasis is no longer on high productivity, which perhaps may now be taken for granted, but on the quality of life, and the song is followed by a recital of the company objectives:

Our purpose shall be not solely to gain wealth nor to display industrial strength; but to contribute to the progress and welfare of the community and the nation ... we shall repay the kindness of our associates, our community, our nation and our foreign friends with gratitude ... Let us provide an abundance of quality electrical appliances to enrich people's lives elsewhere.(14)

Electrical appliances are not necessarily life-enhancing, especially if they are noisy and belong to the people next door, but this is not a serious consideration for the Japanese, who enjoy plenty of noise and excitement anyway, and the domestic market of Matsushita and its competitors is thriving. The Akihabara district of Tokyo is 'Electric City', a cacophonic maze of alleyways, roadside stalls, and multistorey shopping centres selling every kind of electrical goods imaginable, and it does a literally roaring trade. The homes of Japan are now crammed with these products, and there could hardly be a greater contrast than that between the typical Japanese living room and the quiet emptiness of the teahouse. Nevertheless, nearly every home has its 'tokonoma', traditional alcove, with a scroll or picture and a vase of flowers, and the tea ceremony and flower arrangement are still regarded as desirable accomplishments of a girl seeking marriage. Most large companies offer their workers instruction in these ancient arts, and it is part of their paternalism – another legacy of the shoguns – to find the girl a suitable husband should she so wish.

'Alone we are weak, together we are strong. We shall work together as a family in mutual trust and responsibility'. – another verse of the Matsushita creed(14). In many ways, the company is more of a family than the family itself, and the needs of the company frequently take precedence over those of the home. For a business executive, the working day does not end when the factory closes down. Three or four nights a week he will be expected to entertain clients in bars, restaurants and night clubs, and usually he will not arrive home until midnight. At weekends he may practise golf on the company course, or visit a company recreation centre in the country. He will probably spend his annual vacation with a group of his working companions, and when he dies he may even be laid to rest in a company grave.

The paternalism of industry, the loyalty of workers, the social hierarchies apparent in every walk of life, the exchange of business cards, the bowing, the use of 'respect language', the importance attached to meetings and ceremonies – all these aspects of modern Japan may be seen to derive from Confucianism as embodied in *The Legacy of Ieyasu* early in the seventeenth century. Yet, for a true understanding of the Japanese character one must look to the native religion, Shinto. Confucianism was a comparative newcomer, and its main concern was to codify and regulate ways of thought and behaviour already established. But for centuries Shinto had used a concept of hierarchy based on observed realities – though all men were considered virtuous, clearly they were not identical, and it was only realistic to treat one as superior or inferior to another.

Although seeming to be something of an anachronism in the modern city environment, Shinto continues to be a vital force in daily life. A recent survey of religious sects in Japan revealed more than 80,000,000 followers of Shinto, and an almost identical number of devout Buddhists. Since the total population is little more than 110,000,000, it is clear that most people hedge their bets by following both religions at one and the same time. In the majority of homes there are two altars – one for Shinto gods, the kami, and the other for the family dead. When the people get up in the morning, they first clap their hands in worship of the guardian spirits and then burn incense for the souls of the departed. The functions of the two religions are clearly differentiated. Shinto is the religion of life, firmly rooted in the practical realities of day-to-day existence, and people go to Shinto shrines to get married and to celebrate the birth of their children. Shinto places great emphasis on purity and regards death as the ultimate pollution, so when a death occurs in the family, it is a matter not for a Shinto priest but for a Buddhist one. The deceased is buried in a Buddhist cemetery, and never in the precincts of a Shinto shrine.

Of the many different sects of Buddhism still flourishing, it is Zen which has had the most profound effect on cultural life. Through its techniques of meditation and concentration of willpower, it has endowed the people with an extraordinary patience, an ability to remain motionless for hours at a stretch, and a stoic endurance of misery and hardship. In lending its techniques to the martial arts, it made the samurai the most feared warriors in Asia, and when applied to the visual arts, to painting, calligraphy, architecture and landscape gardening, Zen gave form to the artistic ideals of simplicity and restraint which are now regarded throughout the world as characteristically Japanese.

The influence of Zen is undeniable, but it flourished only because it was able to build on foundations firmly laid by Shinto. The Katsura villa in Kyoto, widely regarded as the finest example of Zen-inspired architecture, has much in common with the Grand Shrine of Ise, built a thousand years earlier. The cleanness of line, the sensitivity to texture, and the fastidious avoidance of ostentatious decoration, which are so characteristic of the Zen style, are present also in Shinto architecture reflecting the Shinto love of purity in nature. In looking for the true wellsprings of Japanese thought, temperament and behaviour, it seems that one always comes back to the native religion. 'Shinto, often unrecognizable, is all around us, an invisible fluid running through Japanese society, from the amenities and habits of the home to the essence of artistic taste, from the ways of thinking as expressed in language, to the basic attitudes towards the predicament of man on the planet Earth ... The Japanese, both in work and relaxation, enjoy the mere fact of living to the hilt. They work, like myriads of buzzing bees, with a dedication that can only stem from an undivided and terribly healthy soul. No doubts, caused by the memory of some original sin in the backyard of the collective subconscious, trouble their sleep ... The world is good; work is good; fruits are good; sex is good; and even war is good, provided you win it. All this is entirely consonant with the Spirit of Shinto.'(4)

At the site of Expo '70, the giant face of the sun goddess
looms over an audience of young people at a rock concert, a
symbol of the Japanese spirit in an age of Westernization.

In Himeji, Hideyoshi's magnificent castle towers sublimely over the industrial landscape, having been recently restored at a considerable cost.

Opposite In the centre of Tokyo, a building of the Imperial Palace appears to be overshadowed by the citadels of the merchant class, but this is a trick of the telephoto lens. The palace is well separated from its modern surroundings and maintains its privacy.

Overleaf Osaka castle is lost within the sprawling megalopolis which already stretches far beyond the horizon, and which by the end of the century will probably have swallowed up every inch of available land between here and Tokyo, nearly 400 miles away.

Owing to the mountainous nature of the landscape, 90 per cent
of the population is crowded onto a narrow coastal plain
sandwiched between the Japan Alps and the Pacific Ocean. The
residential areas below the Kyoto hills are more spacious than
most, but even here the houses are packed together and there is
often no more than twelve inches separating one house from another.

In Tokyo, city of a million cars, it is often quicker to walk than to take a taxi. Many streets are cordoned off as pedestrian precincts, and multiple crossings allow people to cross the streets in all directions at once, whilst the traffic waits for them – an idea imported from the United States.

Beside a station in Kyoto, the bicycles of commuters
are neatly packed together, like metallic sardines.
At the end of the day they will be retrieved in an
orderly, disciplined manner – if they can be found.

At the Osaka factory of the Matsushita Electric Industrial
Company, makers of National Panasonic television sets and
Technics Hi Fi, the workers begin the day with a routine of
exercises to instructions which issue from loudspeakers nearby.

Close to its ultramodern assembly lines, the Matsushita
company has constructed a traditional tearoom, where
unmarried girls of the workforce are encouraged to come
at the end of the day for lessons in flower arrangement,
'ikebana'. The tea ceremony and ikebana are still considered
necessary accomplishments for a girl seeking marriage.

Matsushita Konosuke, the founder of the Matsushita company,
recently opened a graduate school to train the political
leaders of the future, and here too there is a tearoom.
Before receiving instruction in the tea ceremony, the school's
student élite bow towards the tokonoma alcove which contains a
scroll with the words of Mr Matsushita himself: 'Be open-minded.'

Before construction begins on their new office building, company
executives in Tokyo attend a Shinto ceremony to consecrate the
ground and secure the goodwill of the local kami, the earth spirits.

With measured steps, a Buddhist monk approaches the Asakusa
Kannon temple in the heart of Tokyo. As he goes, he quietly
chants the holy sutras, and rings a tiny bell to attract the
attention of passers-by. Asakusa temple was founded in the
seventh century and, in the eighteenth century, it stood at the edge
of the notorious pleasure quarter of the Yoshiwara. Today it is
surrounded by shops, bars and striptease parlours. Having been
destroyed in the war, it is now solidly rebuilt in ferroconcrete.

The floats of the Gion festival are festooned with fine
carpets and tapestry, and they carry an orchestra of flutes,
gongs and drums. Cords attached to the instruments hang down
beside the floats and jig up and down as the musicians play.
The Gion festival is almost as old as Kyoto itself. It
originated in 869 and, by the end of the tenth century, it was
already an annual event with much of the splendour it enjoys today.

Opposite In a Kyoto side street, the tenth century meets
the twentieth, as local residents re-assemble the ancient wooden
float which they will trundle through the city in the Gion
festival. Ten tons in weight and 100 feet high, the float must
be manoeuvred out of the street with great care if it is
not to foul the tangle of power cables overhead.

At the front of each float, two leaders with fans give co-ordinating
signals and encouragement to the forty men straining to haul them along.
The designs on their fans and kimonos symbolize the theme of their
particular float. In this case it is the three-day-old crescent moon.

On 17 July, the climax of the festival, enormous crowds
gather to watch and photograph the procession of giant floats, but
the people are so orderly and so respectful of official signs
and barriers that the police have little to do, and they squat
down in the road, careful not to block anyone's view.

The most striking characteristic of the Shinto religion is its
emphasis on purity, and the ancient Shinto rites of purification have
their modern equivalent in the ritual of the hot bath and the obsession
with cleanliness which requires shoes to be removed on entering a
room, and which maintains streets free of litter and cars free of grime.

In Shinto shrines, horoscopes are for sale, printed
on small strips of white paper. When they have been
read, they are tied around a sacred object – in this
case, a tree in the grounds of the Heian shrine.

A newly married couple pose for a picture in front of the shrine building where the wedding ceremony has taken place. The bride wears a hairstyle resembling that of geisha, and an under-kimono of white silk, the colour of mourning, to signify that she is now dead to her family. Though it is by no means unusual for people to marry for love, arranged marriages are still very common, and large companies often consider it their responsibility to find suitable partners for their employees.

In Kyoto the gigantic antique fairs, which annually
invade the grounds of shrines and temples, offer a fascinating
glimpse of contemporary Japanese taste, with a
bewildering mixture of new and old, Western and Oriental.

Every Sunday afternoon, in the shadow of the Olympic stadium, Tokyo
teenagers gather in their hundreds to indulge a group passion for
American rock-and-roll. They create an impression of rebellion and
nonconformity, and their youthful exuberance is a far cry from the
dignified restraint of the tea ceremony. And yet, to a great extent,
even these young people are prisoners of tradition – they organize
themselves in feudal-style hierarchies, they follow the instructions
of their leaders without question, they put the interests of their
group before their own – and when the music stops, they return to
a world created not by Elvis Presley, but by Shogun Tokugawa Ieyasu.

REFERENCES

1 A. L. Sadler, *The Maker of Modern Japan: The Life of Tokugawa Ieyasu* (Charles E. Tuttle, 1979)

2 Yukio Mishima, *Yukio Mishima on 'Hagakure': The Samurai Ethic and Modern Japan* (Penguin Books, 1979)

3 Richard Storry, *The Way of the Samurai* (Orbis Publishing, 1978)

4 Fosco Maraini, *Japan: Patterns of Continuity* (Kodansha International, 1978)

5 G. B. Sansom, *Japan: A Short Cultural History* (Barrie and Jenkins)

6 Donald Keene (ed.), *Anthology of Japanese Literature to the Nineteenth Century* (Penguin Books, 1968)

7 H. Paul Varley, *Japanese Culture: A Short History* (Faber and Faber, 1973)

8 Donald Keene, *No: The Classical Theatre of Japan* (Kodansha International, 1967)

9 Faubion Bowers, *Theatre in the East: A Survey of Asian Dance and Drama* (Thomas Nelson and Sons, 1956)

10 Nakane Chie, *Japanese Society* (Penguin Books, 1973)

11 Ruth Benedict, *The Chrysanthemum and the Sword: Patterns of Japanese Culture* (Charles E. Tuttle)

12 Murray Sayle, 'Japan Style Versus Tokyo Lifestyle'

13 Ivan Morris, *The Nobility of Failure: Tragic Heroes in the History of Japan* (Secker and Warburg, 1975). From an extract in the *Sunday Times* Weekly Review, 23 November 1975

14 *Company Objectives* from Matsushita Company

HISTORICAL TABLE

4–5th century Yamato dynasty (progenitors of present Imperial family) becomes paramount power in Japan.

6th century Introduction of Buddhism.

7th century Adoption of Chinese methods of centralized government by Yamato dynasty.

710 Foundation of Nara, Japan's first permanent capital.

794 Establishment of new capital of Heian (later known as Kyoto).

858 Beginning of two centuries of domination over Imperial court and government by regents from the aristocratic Fujiwara family.

1156–60 Political rivalry in Kyoto leads to armed conflict involving samurai and results in domination by Taira clan.

1180–5 Defeat of the Taira by the Minamoto in the Gempei War.

1185 The Minamoto leader, Yoritomo, establishes a military administration at Kamakura.

1192 Title of Shogun conferred on Yoritomo by emperor.

1274 First Mongol invasion repulsed.

1281 Second Mongol invasion repulsed.

14th century Development of noh drama under Ashikaga patronage.

1333 Overthrow of Kamakura Shogunate by rival warrior clans.

1336–92 Imperial family split into rival 'Northern' and 'Southern' courts as war among samurai leaders spreads.

1338 Ashikaga Takauji, a powerful military leader, becomes Shogun.

1467 Onin War sparks off over a century of feudal warfare known as the Sengoku period.

1542 Birth of Tokugawa Ieyasu.

1543 Arrival of first Europeans (Portuguese).

1568 Oda Nobunaga, with support from Ieyasu, gains control of Kyoto.

1573 End of Ashikaga Shogunate.

1582 Betrayal and assassination of Nobunaga by Akechi Mitsuhide.

1585 Nobunaga's leading general and effective successor, Toyotomi Hideyoshi, reaches understanding with Ieyasu.

1590 Hideyoshi achieves hegemony.

1598 Death of Hideyoshi.

1600 Ieyasu and his feudal supporters triumph in battle of Sekigahara.

1603 Ieyasu's claim to be Shogun ratified by emperor. Tokugawa (or Edo) period begins.

1605 Ieyasu 'retires' nominally as Shogun in favour of son Hidetada.

1615 Destruction of remaining opposition to Tokugawa by capture of Osaka castle.

1616 Death of Ieyasu.

1623 'Retirement' of Hidetada as Shogun in favour of son Iemitsu.

1636–41 Closure of Japan to almost all foreign contact.

1688–1704 Urban culture flowers in Genroku era.

1701–3 The 47 Ronin incident.

1720s Tokugawa Shogunate begins to encounter serious financial problems.

1853 Arrival of Commodore Perry seeking the re-opening of Japan.

1868 Tokugawa Shogunate overthrown in name of revival of Imperial rule (Meiji Restoration).

1870s Enthusiasm for Bummei Kaika ('Civilization and Enlightenment' from the West).

1871 Abolition of feudal domains.

1876 Ban on wearing of swords ends period of special status for samurai.

GLOSSARY

Amae Dependence on a particular superior from whom support, and to some extent indulgence, is expected, rather as a child expects this from parents.

Bugaku Ancient stately court dances, originally introduced from China and Korea in the seventh and eighth centuries, in which the performers, often wearing masks, mime to the accompaniment of ceremonial music (gagaku).

Bunraku The most common name for the Japanese theatrical genre in which the parts are played by puppets, each of which is manipulated by a main operator and two assistants, while the story is chanted to the accompaniment of the samisen.

Bushido 'The way of the warrior', the samurai ethical code which emphasized bravery, self-discipline, propriety, frugality, simplicity and, above all, absolute loyalty to one's lord.

Chonin 'Townspeople', the non-samurai population of the cities and towns of pre-modern Japan, particularly the merchants.

Daimyo The feudal lords who, through their samurai retainers, controlled most areas of Japan, usually under either the hegemony or the nominal overlordship of a shogun, between the fourteenth and nineteenth centuries.

Denkaku A primitive form of dance with musical accompaniment originally associated with the seeking of divine favour at the time of planting rice.

Eta The inhabitants of special communities who were traditionally regarded by other Japanese as unclean or tainted, probably because as tanners, butchers, etc. their work involved the killing of animals. Now known usually as burakumin and numbering about two million, they still suffer discrimination in practice, even though their legal status was made the same as that of ordinary Japanese in 1871.

Gagaku Ancient form of music, often accompanied by stately dancing or mime, which was introduced from Korea and T'ang China and is still performed at Imperial court ceremonies and at some shrines and temples on appropriate occasions.

Geisha Highly skilled and very expensive female entertainer trained from an early age in the arts of singing, dancing, conversation and making guests relax.

Gigaku Ancient form of music, accompanied by masked dancing, deriving from India, Tibet or China, and introduced into Japan from Korea in the seventh century.

Gimu Unconditional obligation or duty.

Giri That which is right or just or proper or reasonable; moral obligation, debt of gratitude, duty.

Harakiri 'Cutting the belly', the ritual of self-disembowelment first clearly recorded in twelfth-century Japan. As well as becoming the customary form of execution of sumurai, it was also, in extreme cases, a way of preserving a samurai's honour or protesting against injustice.

Joruri The chanting of dramatic ballads to samisen accompaniment which in the seventeenth century combined with the manipulation of puppets to form the theatrical genre which came to be known as bunraku.

Kabuki Popular and colourful Japanese dramatic form incorporating dance and music which emerged in the seventeenth century from somewhat disreputable origins.

Kami A word often translated as 'god', but which originally referred more diffusely to many things or persons regarded as superior, such as mountains or dead heroes and rulers, as well as to anything which was dreaded or revered.

Kamikaze 'Divine wind', a term frequently used for the typhoon which dispersed the Mongol invasion fleet in 1281, and more recently applied to the suicidal Japanese pilots who attempted to crash their planes onto American ships in the final stages of the Pacific War.

Kana The Japanese phonetic symbols, of which seventy-one are now in common use, which were developed during the eighth and ninth centuries by simplifying Chinese ideographs with the same sound.

Kirisute-gomen The right enjoyed by samurai to cut down and leave where he lay a commoner who insulted him or showed disrespect.

Koku A traditional measurement of quantity, particularly for rice. One koku was equivalent to just under five bushels (about 300 lb.).

Maiko 'Dancing-girl', a pupil geisha in her last stage of training.

Meishi A card indicating the name, address, status and company or institution of its bearer. Such cards are carried by large numbers of Japanese men and not a few women, and are exchanged on first meeting.

Miyabi Elegance and refinement – a quality highly esteemed in traditional Japanese culture.

Mono no aware A phrase in classical Japanese literature that expressed the sense of poignance and transience of life which was felt particularly acutely when the changing seasons and the beauties of nature were contemplated and when scenes of past happiness were recalled.

Munen 'No-thought', a Zen Buddhist term which refers to the state of mind achieved when a skill has been so thoroughly mastered by discipline that actions flow spontaneously without being hindered by any doubt or consciousness of technical problems.

Ninjo 'Human feelings', a term which points to the more natural emotional side of the Japanese character. The conflict between human feelings and duty (giri) has been an important theme in Japanese drama and literature.

Noh A word meaning 'accomplishment' or 'performance' which came to refer to the classical dramatic form developed by Kanami and Zeami in the fourteenth century. The actors wear masks and move in a highly stylized manner to the accompaniment of a chanted chorus and music from flutes and drums.

Nimmu Duty to one's work.

Oiran A word for a courtesan or high-class prostitute which dates back at least to the Tokugawa period.

On : oya on, shi no on, nushi no on A word which basically means 'kindness' or 'a favour', but also carries the further implication of 'debt of gratitude' or 'obligation'.

Onnagata The female roles in Kabuki, which since the seventeenth century have always been played by men. The term also refers to the actors who specialize in playing women.

Ronin Literally 'wave-men', a term applied to samurai who had lost or left their lord, usually as a result of defeat in battle.

Sabi Literally 'rust', but a word which also

conveys the sense of 'antique-looking archaic imperfection', and unpretentious rusticity, qualities highly esteemed in the Zen aesthetic approach.

Sake Rice-wine, Japan's traditional alcoholic drink, usually drunk warm.

Samisen A three-stringed, banjo-like instrument, which was introduced from south China in the sixteenth century and became common as an accompaniment for popular ballads and in the theatre.

Samurai The warriors (often called bushi) who originally were probably members or retainers of dominant local families in Japan and whose members and importance increased as the power of the central government declined between the ninth and twelfth centuries. In early times most samurai fought on horseback with bow and arrows, which they were able to shoot while riding, and a curved sword, but in later years many also fought on foot, and the wearing of two swords became common.

Sarugaku Literally 'monkey music', a form of dancing with music, probably derived from the kagura dances, which are performed at Shinto festivals and eventually contributed to the emergence of noh drama and to the comic interludes (called kyogen) between noh plays.

Sensei The normal word for 'teacher', but may also be used to show respect to an older person.

Seppuku The more literary, Chinese-style, reading of the ideographs usually pronounced harakari.

Shinto 'The way of the kami', the primitive religion of Japan. Basically it was the nature worship of an agrarian people to whom fertility

and purification rites were important. There seems also to have been an emphasis on reverence for the ancestral deity of the uji (clan) to which families belonged, and also on obedience to the uji chief.

Shogun A title, meaning 'Barbarian-conquering Great General', granted by the emperor to the feudal leader Minamoto Yoritomo in 1192, and held thereafter by the heads of the Ashikaga and Tokugawa families, who both achieved hegemony over their rivals and were able to claim Minamoto ancestry.

Shogunate The government of a shogun (in Japanese, bakufu).

Shoya A village headman.

Tachi A long sword.

Tayu A high-class prostitute or courtesan.

Terakoya The term, meaning 'temple hut' originally, which came to be applied, because of the importance of Buddhist priests in developing commoner education, to all of the approximately fifteen thousand village schools which had been established by the end of the Tokugawa period (1867).

Tokonama An elevated alcove in a corner of a room where a scroll would be hung or some other ornament displayed.

Ukiyo 'The floating world', a phrase of Buddhist origin which came to be used in the late seventeenth century to describe the many new features and fashions of city life.

Ukiyoe The wood-block prints, at first in black and white but later multi-coloured, which from the mid seventeenth century depicted scenes and personalities from the 'floating world' of Edo and Osaka. They especially feature g sha,

courtesans and actors.

Wabi A term, meaning 'acceptance of simplicity' and 'austerity', which expresses an approach to life in accord with Zen attitudes.

Wabi-cha The style of conducting the tea ceremony which emphasizes simple elegance and a quiet, reverent atmosphere, and which has been the accepted approach since the time of Sen no Rikyu in the sixteenth century.

Wakizashi A short sword.

Wakon-yosai 'Japanese spirit – Western skills', a slogan used by those conservative reformers in the late nineteenth century, who wanted to introduce modern technology and science from the West while preserving Japanese ethical, social and political values.

Yugen A term which embraces profundity, mystery, and subtlety, qualities which, under Zen influence, were highly esteemed in literature and especially in noh drama.

Zaibatsu The huge industrial-financial combines, usually controlled by a holding company, which dominated the modern sectors of the Japanese economy before 1945.

Zen Buddhism A sect introduced from China in the twelfth century, which was patronized by feudal leaders under both the Minamoto and Ashikaga shogunates. Its emphasis on mental and physical self-disipline appealed to many samurai as did its stress on meditation and inner enlightenment rather than sutras. Zen austerity and ambiguity had a very considerable influence on Japanese art and literature, but its adherents have never been so numerous as those of several other Buddhist sects in Japan.

ACKNOWLEDGEMENTS

Many of the photographs in this book were taken during BBC filming, and I am indebted to BBC cameramen Colin Waldeck, David Whitson and David Feig for permitting me to take advantage of their professional skills in lighting; to their assistants David Bennett, John Sennett and Anthony Bragg, for many a good suggestion of camera angle; and to sound recordists Dave Jewitt, Bob Roberts and Ian Sansam, for gently advising when camara clicks were tolerable and when not.

I would like to take this opportunity to thank Ian Mutsu who, ten years ago, encouraged me to extend a two-week visit to Japan into one of six months, and in doing so effectively laid the foundations for this book. In making films, as in taking photographs, the foreigner in Japan is totally dependent on his interpreters; and I am deeply grateful to Kenji Arai, interpreter for the films *Japanese George*, *Ustinov at Expo 70*, and *Music of a Thousand Autumns*, and to Yasuhiro Kano, who worked on *The Shogun Inheritance*, for their prodigious energy and enthusiasm, and their wholehearted involvement in our projects.

My thanks are due also to NTV, the Japanese co-producers of *The Shogun Inheritance*; to Toshio Yokoyama, for telling me about the little-known Kaseda festival, and for his advice on cultural matters

in general; and to the many people who appear in this book, and who extended to the BBC team the hospitality and kindness for which Japan is renowned.

In the technical field I would like to express my gratitude to the Nikon company for the loan of their magnificent 300mm. F2.8 ED lens, responsible for the photographs of Kabuki and Bunraku in this book; and to Leitz, Japan, for their rapid servicing of my Leica cameras.

Closer to home, I offer my thanks to Sue Henny of the Japan Foundation, for generously sharing her knowledge of Japan and for providing me with a comprehensive reading list; to Sue Haycock, researcher on *The Shogun Inheritance* film series, for permitting me to delve into her excellent and colourful notes; to Victor Harris at the British Museum, for his help in selecting wood-block prints to introduce our chapters; to Dr Richard Sims for scholarly advice; and finally, to the professional team responsible for this book – to the editor, Robin Baird-Smith, for his patience and attention to detail, to Ron Clark for a most discerning eye in the selection of photographs, and to the designer Charles Elton, for his skill and judgement in putting it all together, and for giving my photographs the chance to look their best.